T0079265

George Bernard Shaw: A Very Short Introduction

VERY SHORT INTRODUCTIONS are for anyone wanting a stimulating and accessible way into a new subject. They are written by experts, and have been translated into more than 45 different languages.

The series began in 1995, and now covers a wide variety of topics in every discipline. The VSI library currently contains over 650 volumes—a Very Short Introduction to everything from Psychology and Philosophy of Science to American History and Relativity—and continues to grow in every subject area.

Very Short Introductions available now:

Available soon:

For more information visit our website

www.oup.com/vsi/

Christopher Wixson

GEORGE BERNARD SHAW

A Very Short Introduction

OXFORD
UNIVERSITY PRESS

Great Clarendon Street, Oxford, OX2 6DP,
United Kingdom

Oxford University Press is a department of the University of Oxford.
It furthers the University's objective of excellence in research, scholarship,
and education by publishing worldwide. Oxford is a registered trade mark of
Oxford University Press in the UK and in certain other countries

© Christopher Wixson 2020

The moral rights of the author have been asserted

First edition published in 2020

Impression: 1

Published in the United States of America by Oxford University Press
198 Madison Avenue, New York, NY 10016, United States of America

British Library Cataloguing in Publication Data
Data available

Library of Congress Control Number: 2019951497

ISBN 978-0-19-885009-0

Printed in Great Britain by
Ashford Colour Press Ltd, Gosport, Hampshire

Contents

Acknowledgements

My ongoing intellectual engagement with Bernard Shaw and his writing has been informed and inspired by the brilliant and substantive work of generations of scholars, especially Austin Briggs, Ronald Bryden, L. W. Conolly, Tracy Davis, Richard Dietrich, Bernie Dukore, Peter Gahan, J. Ellen Gainor, A. M. Gibbs, Nicholas Grene, Dan H. Laurence, Margery Morgan, Sally Peters, Jean Reynolds, Nelson O'Ceallaigh Ritschel, Joan Templeton, and Stanley Weintraub. They have been my teachers, and their collective insight has enhanced significantly the learning experience of decades of my own students.

I would be remiss in not acknowledging the profound influence of nearly forty years of theatregoing at the Shaw Festival in Niagara-on-the-Lake, Ontario, Canada, which season after season makes Shaw's plays speak from the contemporary stage compellingly, movingly, and resonantly.

Enormous thanks to the hardworking and proficient staff at Oxford University Press, particularly Senior Commissioning Editor Andrea Keegan, Senior Assistant Commissioning Editor Jenny Nugee, editorial assistant Christina Fleischer, Senior Picture Researcher Deborah Protheroe, and two anonymous readers.

I am also sincerely grateful for the ongoing enthusiasm and support from colleagues, friends, and family: Melissa Ames; Kevin Doolen; Tim Engles; Anne Thibault Geen; Linda Peete; Tim Taylor; Angela Vietto; Neal, Donna, and Lindsey Wixson; and Roland, Lois, and Valerie Worthington.

Finally, I continue to be deeply indebted to Marjorie Worthington and Maisie, Charlie, and Callie Wixson, who nourish me in myriad ways every day. Our journey together is such a stirringly big adventure.

George Bernard Shaw

List of illustrations

Introduction: 'Shavian'

In 2016, when American singer and songwriter Bob Dylan was awarded the Nobel Prize in Literature, commentators were quick to point out that he simultaneously joined an even more exclusive club, laureates who also have earned an Oscar. The only other member is George Bernard Shaw, and neither one was too comfortable with the prestigious international recognition. The Swedish Academy had enormous difficulty trying to get a hold of Dylan, who finally contacted them a couple weeks after the public announcement saying he was honoured but would not attend the lavish award ceremony. Similarly ambivalent, Shaw only reluctantly accepted (at the behest of his wife) but refused the prize money. He felt that he could 'forgive Alfred Nobel for inventing dynamite, but only a fiend in human form could have invented the Nobel Prize'. While the fruits of both artists' creative labour have been called 'word-music', for Fintan O'Toole, Shaw's most recent chronicler, their affinity runs deeper in that each is 'one of the great masters of self-invention, a nobody who captured the zeitgeist':

> Shaw was one of the first private individuals on the planet to fully understand how to generate—and how to use—global fame. He was among the first private citizens to grasp the possibilities of mass media and the age of mechanical reproduction for the creation of a different kind of power in the world. He was one of the first to

understand that, in this mass-media age, performance is not just what happens on the stage, it is everywhere.

Shaw was at heart a consummate performer, and his meticulous curating of his 'GBS' persona across platforms of all kinds made him one of the world's most recognizable public intellectuals and literary figures throughout much of his long life (Figure 1).

Shaw was compulsively drawn to controversy. When he didn't start them, he fed them, galvanized by how eagerly they made people talk, hopefully listen, and ideally motivated to live more intentionally and equitably. Indeed, it was that fervent commitment to substantive verbal exchange that enabled Shaw, beginning in the 1890s, to transform British drama, bringing to it intellectual substance, ethical imperatives, and modernity itself, setting the theatrical course for the subsequent century. He rejected a view of the stage as primarily a showcase for spectacle and a showroom for escapism, deploring plays that intentionally avoided direct engagement with the outside world and instead traded in puerile, claptrap conventions of character and plot. With his criticism and later his style of playwriting, he fought to realize his vision of the theatre as a sacred space in which ideas and social issues could be discussed in compelling, provocative ways. With a canon of plays astonishing in size, breadth, and ambition, Shaw is considered by many to be the second greatest playwright in English behind William Shakespeare.

In a private residence on Upper Synge Street in Dublin, the son of George Carr and Lucinda Elizabeth Gurly Shaw arrived in the world on 26 July 1856. But, he might point puckishly to a second, equally momentous birthday, that of the unique adjective that denotes both definitive characteristics of Shaw's work, views, and ideas and those disciples who embrace and celebrate them. Continuing in wide usage today, the word 'Shavian' first appeared in print on 2 November 1904, marking the full germination of Shaw's 'GBS' persona, when the *Times* critic Arthur Bingham

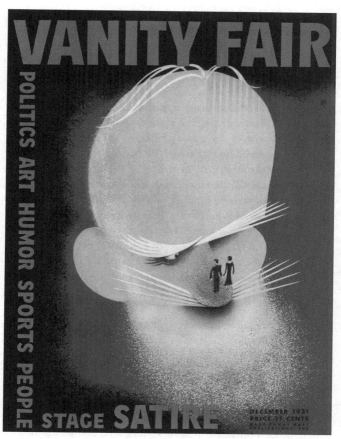

1. *Vanity Fair* cover (**December 1931**).

Walkley referred to Shaw's play *John Bull's Other Island* as a 'thoroughly Shavian farrago'. What it is to be Shavian though is itself often figured as paradox. In 1944, the *Saturday Review* quipped that 'the only certainty about [Shaw] has always been that he will be different; the only predictable feature that he will be unpredictable'. Yet, there never was any mistaking the singular

3

voice and style of GBS, and the task of this volume is to sketch in the contours of what constitutes 'Shavian'.

George Bernard Shaw: A Very Short Introduction provides an accessible foundation for those discovering Shaw's writing for the first time, on the page or on the stage, and provides a framework for further study and deepened appreciation. The sheer verbosity and scope of Shaw's writing can at times feel daunting; indeed, there are few writers who are so prolific, so interdisciplinary, so audacious, *and* who lived so long. This book is not meant to substitute for the experience of reading or seeing productions of Shaw's plays nor will it offer either detailed summaries of them or a thorough, extensive biography of their author. Rather, with many opportunities to encounter Shaw 'in his own words', it will sketch the creative evolution of core themes and styles over his long career. While far from exhaustive on its subject, this volume offers an overview of Shaw's sensibility as a writer and public figure so as to foster among readers and audience members greater confidence in joining the conversations he orchestrates.

The book is organized into seven chapters. The first, '"GBS"', investigates Shaw's early years in Dublin, the forging of his professional roots in London, and the contriving of his impish, fearless public persona. The remaining six chapters are each titled with an adjective Shaw himself selected to organize and characterize the published versions of his plays. They each stand for linchpin Shavian elements that together are always simultaneously operative in Shaw's critical and dramaturgical practice. Both '"Unpleasant"' and '"Pleasant"' examine the first decade of his career as a dramatist (the 1890s). '"Puritan"' focuses upon Shaw's moulding of stage comedy at the dawning of the 20th century to dramatize the workings of his emerging religion. '"Political"' details a difficult time in the playwright's career when his views about the First World War placed him intensely at odds with public opinion but from which eventually emerge his greatest plays and highest accolades. Tracing the final phase of his dramaturgy, '"Extravagant"' attends to the ways in which his plays continue to experiment with dramatic form as he looks for ways to recover his optimism in social progress amid the devastating effects of the war and economic depression. Lastly, '"Farfetched"' charts the contours of the end of Shaw's life and his own sense of his legacy.

Fearlessly provocative on both existential and socio-political questions, Shaw as GBS went viral across international stages and screens, across the pages of newspapers and periodicals, and across the airwaves via radio and television. As such, his polemical style of activism anticipates that particular mode of witty iconoclasm emulated by cable news pundits and social media influencers in 21st-century culture. That his celebrity brand endures, seventy years after his death, is testament to the prescience of his thinking, the distinctiveness of his style, and his unflagging commitment to the physics of words in performance and the play of conversation. Editions of his plays have been classroom staples for decades, productions of them fixtures on regional, university, and national stages throughout North America, Britain, and the world, including at the annual Shaw Festival (established in 1962) in Niagara-on-the-Lake, Ontario, Canada. The resilient ability of Shaw's writing not only to survive but *adapt* in dialogue with the evolution of technologized global culture, changing trends and movements within academic scholarship, and current styles and innovations in theatrical practice is impressively striking and energizing for Shavians all over the world. Indeed, as playwright J. B. Priestley noted on the occasion of the centenary of the playwright's birth, 'some of the air we breathe now has GBS in it'.

Chapter 1
'GBS'

In later life, fashioning an origin story for GBS predicated upon superhuman self-improvement and the triumph over mediocre circumstances, Shaw would write disparagingly about his father, his parents' marriage and 1873 separation, and his childhood in general, spent in what he called 'shabby genteel poverty'. Allegedly, his mother's family, disappointed at her choice of husband, disinherited her while his father, a corn merchant member of the Protestant Ascendancy, struggled professionally and personally. Shaw would quip that he was a 'downstart and the son of a downstart' and so disliked his given name—his father's—that he would routinely sign documents 'G. Bernard Shaw'. Yet, while he would often belie the extent of their influence, his earliest experiences sowed the seeds of that distinctive political and artistic Shavian sensibility.

Dublin

A bright but restless boy, Shaw's youth was characterized by nomadic schooling, at which he was a proficient if disgruntled student, attending four different schools in seven years before abandoning it to become a clerk in a land-agent office at the age of 15. In that capacity, Shaw proved himself adept at budgeting and managing money and forged a thriftiness that would persist even after his remarkable financial success. The antipathy towards formal schooling that resulted from those early experiences instilled in him another lifelong habit—self-directed learning—which began at this time through avid reading, frequent visits to the National Gallery of Ireland, habitually attending performances at Dublin's Theatre Royal, and his thorough absorption in music. His mother nursed ambitions to become a singer and achieved notoriety as a Dublin vocalist, and her musical tutor, George Vandeleur Lee (who actually lived with the family for seven years), exerted an enormous effect on the curious boy and would later help establish him as a professional critic. Unsurprisingly, considering he was born into a family in which everyone (including extended relations) played an instrument, the young Shaw quickly became a baritone vocalist, self-taught pianist, and proficient whistler 'from end to end [of] leading works of Handel, Haydn, Mozart, Beethoven, Rossini, Bellini, Donizetti, and Verdi'. Their influence was especially profound on his eventual craft as a playwright in which he 'scored' stage voices; 'my method, my system, my tradition', he would later claim, 'is founded upon music'. With regard to his cultivation and promotion of his 'GBS' public persona, he would credit Handel for teaching him that 'style consists in a force of assertion'.

In addition, growing up adjacent to sordid tenement districts rife with disease and inhabited by a population decimated by famine, illiteracy, and unemployment, the young Shaw was confronted daily by shocking suffering and discrimination conducted along religious, class, and political lines. 'Poverty', he would write in *Major Barbara* (1905), is 'the worst of crimes. All the other crimes are virtues beside it; all the other dishonors are chivalry itself by comparison.' In many ways, the Ireland of his youth starkly delineated the barriers that inhibited individual attainment, meaningful discussion, and collective advancement, which he eventually would spend his entire professional life trying to eradicate. All the various facets of his childhood together equipped him with the means to do so—moral indignation at the living and working conditions of the poor and empathy for all those disadvantaged by social hierarchies combined with a comprehensive grounding in the arts to set the stage for his becoming one of the world's most celebrated pundits. However, he would not return to the city of his upbringing until he and his wife began a series of tours through the country in the early decades of the new century.

London

In his early twenties, despite being offered a promotion and a raise in salary that would clinch his establishment in a respectable and lucrative line of work, Shaw resigned from the land-agent office, claiming not to have enough to do to justify the increased pay. Leaving his father and Ireland behind in the spring of 1876, Shaw went to live in London with his mother and his sister Lucy. To support the household, Mrs. Shaw cobbled together some meagre inherited funds, modest weekly contributions from her husband, and earnings as Vandeleur Lee's assistant and from both private and public school lessons. In the meantime, her ambitious son spent an enormous amount of time in the reading room at the British Museum as well as attending public lectures and meetings. In 1879, he took a job that tasked him with going door to door and trying to convince homeowners to install rooftop towers to support Edison Company telephone wires. In response to lacklustre results, the company shifted him to a salaried position and eventually promoted him to management. But he quit after less than a year, much more interested in continuing his voracious self-education and hoping to establish himself as a writer.

Inspired by a speech given in 1882 by American reformer Henry George, Shaw read a translation of *Das Kapital*, and Karl Marx's seminal economic critique became a cornerstone of his own political thinking, later to be fully articulated in *The Intelligent Woman's Guide to Socialism and Capitalism* (1928). Where he diverged from Marx had to do with the engine of reform; the pacifist recoiled at the notion of violent overthrow as a requirement for progress. He was drawn instead to models of social change achieved steadily by degrees within existing structures and institutions and, in 1884, joined a Socialist group called the Fabian Society, named after a prudent Roman general called Quintus Fabius Maximus. If the Society's agenda was radical in counteracting the oppression of the class and gender system, industrial capitalism, and political disenfranchisement, their methods were not revolutionary. Instead, they were committed activists waging a campaign of words, through published pamphlets as well as public oratory, to spur the *gradual* implementation of collective ownership of resources, income equality, protective labour laws, and other infrastructural reforms by persuading the minds of the voters. Their ideas laid the groundwork for the British Labour Party, and the group's initial leaders (including Shaw) founded the London School of Economics.

Taking up the mantle of public advocacy, the young Shaw rapidly became a sought-after and captivating tract writer, speech giver, debater, and activist crusader on behalf of a variety of social causes, including public health, the status of women, and poverty, all issues that would eventually secure a prominent presence in his plays. In 1881, Shaw committed to vegetarianism, initially in emulation of Percy Bysshe Shelley, whose writing he had devoured as a teenager and who exerted an enormous influence over Shaw's thinking, particularly his sharp views on bourgeois morality and organized religion. The 'birth' of his persona 'GBS' is reputed to have occurred at a meeting of the Shelley Society when Shaw publicly declared himself to be, 'like Shelley, a Socialist, an Atheist, and a Vegetarian'. Coupled with his teetotalism and aversion to smoking, he maintained his diet for the rest of his life and frequently remarked upon how it served both his frugality and vitality, even as he cautioned against idealizing its curative propensities.

Shaw's eating habits were a particular public fascination and a ubiquitous topic for interviewers and even for those who disagreed politically with him. GBS leveraged that interest into a platform from which he could weigh in on everything from animal welfare and the 'murderous absurdity' of the medical-industrial complex to societal debates over public hygiene, mental fitness, and the creation of a nationalized health service. Vegetarian restaurants in London often served as meeting places for reform groups of various kinds and tended to attract individuals from all social classes who shared anti-conventional affinities. Shaw during this time was very active in seeking out organizations that reflected and nourished his emergent beliefs, always keen to be, as the English actor Maurice Colbourne put it, 'an "Ist" or an "Ite" or an "Anti" of some sort'. To further distinguish himself, he stylized his physical appearance with what would become GBS trademarks—the reddish-brown beard and the woollen Jaeger suit, the first of which he purchased with the insurance money he received following the death of his father in April 1885 (Figure 2). His individual studying as well as attendance at functions and demonstrations sponsored by various clubs and societies (most of which he joined) not only continued to hone his beliefs but fostered entanglements in various romantic affairs, including one with Karl Marx's daughter Eleanor. Shaw quickly became a popular and effective Fabian orator, later estimating that he 'delivered upwards of two thousand speeches' around the city during this time, for which he never charged fees. By 1891, as the *Sunday World* put it,

> Everybody in London knows Shaw. Fabian, Socialist, art and musical critic, vegetarian, ascetic, humourist, artist to the tips of his fingers, man of the people to the tips of his boots. The most original and inspiring of men—fiercely uncompromising, full of ideas, irrepressibly brilliant.

GBS had arrived and, for the next half century, would work tirelessly and industriously for meaningful social change. As Shaw would later put it, 'the reasonable man adapts himself to the world: the unreasonable one persists in trying to adapt the

2. 'George Bernard Shaw' (1888), by Sir Emery Walker.

world to himself. Therefore all progress depends on the
unreasonable man.'

Art and music

In between authoring Fabian tracts, Shaw also penned five novels
between 1879 and 1883 (*Immaturity*, *The Irrational Knot*, *Love
Among the Artists*, *Cashel Byron's Profession*, and *An Unsocial
Socialist*). Unfortunately, while all but one appeared in serial
form in various socialist magazines between 1884 and 1888 and
although one (*Cashel Byron's Profession*) was actually rather
popular, the novels failed to attract wider readership at that time
or commitments from publishers anxious over the novelty of their
form and unconventionality of their content. In retrospect, all five
provide insight into Shaw's developing facilities as a writer and

together form a sketch book of sorts, housing experiments with characterizations and situations that he would later sharpen to significant effect for the stage. Much more lucrative in terms of income and professional notice were his stints for a number of periodicals as an often vituperative art, music, book, and drama reviewer, starting in the 1870s with a bit of ghostwriting for Vandeleur Lee in *The Hornet*. In the mid-1880s, his friend William Archer got him started as an art critic for *The World* where, although he appreciated the work of Michelangelo and Pre-Raphaelite painters, he particularly extolled the controversial work of the French Impressionists. Later, Shaw would synthesize many of his musings about exhibitions he attended into his extended published essay *The Sanity of Art* (1895).

Archer would also secure other freelance jobs for him, including one as a reviewer of popular fiction and non-fiction for the *Pall Mall Gazette* and another as music critic for *The World*. Soon after, Shaw began writing clever music reviews for *The Star* under the pseudonym 'Corno di Bassetto', the Italian word for the 18th-century basset horn. His approach was savagely witty and decidedly populist, a revolt against the current tone of music criticism that Shaw felt was high-minded, snobbish, and academic. He would reflect later in life upon Bassetto's lively style as a 'mixture of triviality, vulgarity, farce, and tomfoolery with genuine criticism'. Around the time of his wedding in the late 1890s, Shaw would complete an extended 'commentary' on *The Ring of the Nibelung* called *The Perfect Wagnerite* (1898), analysing and praising Richard Wagner's multi-part saga not only as a piece of music but as an allegorical critique of industrial capitalism. Faulting the cycle's anti-Semitism and the facile remedy it proposes to the social ills it reveals, he would later revise the essay to interpret the opera further as a philosophical text within the context of his own developing theory of Creative Evolution. By 1889, he had contributed upwards of 600 reviews to various periodicals in both the popular and radical press and, by 1890, was ready to start signing his *World* pieces with the initials 'GBS'.

Journalism

For Shaw, journalism represented a privileged opportunity to inform, inspire, and provoke readers directly. In *The Sanity of Art*, he wrote against 'journalists who openly profess that it is their duty to "reflect" what they believe to be the ignorance and prejudice of their readers, instead of leading and enlightening them to the best of their ability'. He saw in the role a chance to shape public opinion so, in addition to promoting new artistic aesthetics, he frequently used reviews to agitate about social issues about which he felt passionate, including censorship, child exploitation, animal vivisection, women's equality, and public health. Importantly, Shaw's emergence in print coincided with the advent of New Journalism, a late 19th-century evolution of tone and style anchored in the charismatic subjectivity of the writer's persona rather than the objectivity of traditional reporting. He also was ingenious at extending the reach of his journalism to different demographics, notably contributing commentaries on boxing to the sports page and even product endorsements in the advert section. Thus, in addition to his speaking activities, the myriad pieces of his writing that appeared regularly in radical and mainstream press outlets served to develop and sharpen Shaw's distinctive rhetorical style—a mesmerizing way with words that is articulate, vigorous, playful, and, above all, opinionated.

Letters to the editor also became a frequent vehicle for his crusading, often critiquing the sensational press coverage of major events. Following the sinking of the *Titanic* in 1912, for example, 'Shaw's journalistic response', as scholar Nelson O'Ceallaigh Ritschel puts it, 'brought reason to the calamity and began the rational process of addressing the causes in a quest to prevent a repeat scenario, [squarely facing] the realities about the sinking, not awash in heroic actions and heroes, but replete in industrial greed and incompetence that led to many needless deaths'.

He was deliberately but not gratuitously provocative with the positions he staked in the press. 'It is always necessary,' he believed,

> to overstate a case startlingly to make people sit up and listen to it, and to frighten them into acting on it. I do this myself habitually and deliberately.

When, in 1888, Jack the Ripper was terrorizing East London and receiving extensive newspaper coverage for his series of gruesome murders, Shaw began a letter that appeared in *The Star* by praising the 'success of the Whitechapel murderer' in calling attention to the horrific poverty of that area of the city, whereas efforts on the part of Fabian activists to do so through traditional channels had failed:

George Bernard Shaw

> Whilst we conventional Social Democrats were wasting our time on education, agitation, and organization, some independent genius has taken the matter in hand, and by simply murdering and disembowelling four women, converted the proprietary press to an inept sort of communism.

He specifically refers to the upsurge in charity contributions that flowed as a result of newspaper accounts of Whitechapel squalor. Ultimately, Shaw's target in this letter is what he calls

> one of the worst curses of poverty[:] these abominable bastard Utopias of genteel charity in which the poor are the first to be robbed and then pauperized by way of compensation, in order that the rich man may combine the idle luxury of the protected thief with the unctuous self-satisfaction of the pious philanthropist.

Just imagine, he further suggests,

> if the habits of duchesses only admitted of their being decoyed into Whitechapel back-yards, a single experiment in slaughterhouse anatomy on an aristocratic victim might fetch in a round half

million and save the necessity of sacrificing four women of
the people.

Rather than relying upon 'a policy of terror' such as the Ripper's
'private enterprise' and the resulting 'gush of bazaars and blood
money', Shaw argues that proper rents ought to be collected
from 'monopolists' by the state and put towards 'the capital of
productive industries for the better employment of the poor'.
For the rest of his career, Shaw made sure GBS was a fixture in
public commentary, regularly contributing letters opining on
newsworthy incidents as well as the day-to-day workings of local
and national politics, and, before too long, press outlets would just
as regularly seek him out for his perspectives as part of their
standard coverage of current events in all fields.

Theatre

Building upon a brief turn for *The Dramatic Review*, Shaw's
critical purview expanded in 1894 to include the theatre when
he began reviewing plays for *The Saturday Review of Politics,
Literature, Science, and Art*, continuing to cultivate his audacious,
wisecracking persona in ridiculing what he deemed a dangerously
outmoded and tedious set of performance conventions and the
commercialized corruption of the stage. He sought to redeem the
theatre as 'a factory of thought, a prompter of conscience, an
elucidator of social conduct, an armory against despair and
dullness, and a temple of the Ascent of Man'. Most urgent was for
drama and its criticism to re-establish a vital link between what
happened on the stage and what was going on around it in the
lived experience of its audiences and practitioners. In an 1895
Saturday Review piece on a production of William Shakespeare's
Twelfth Night, he wrote:

> My real aim is to widen the horizon of the critic, especially of the
> dramatic critic, whose habit at present is to bring a large experience
> of stage life to bear on a scanty experience of real life, although it is

certain that all criticism of the drama must bring a wide and
practical knowledge of real life to bear on the stage.

According to Shaw, theatrical performances should not be treated
as mere escapist amusement by those who produce them or those
who attend them; in 1897, he complained in the *Saturday Review*
of lately having 'suffered...from seeing Shakespeare butchered
to make a cockney's holiday'. He disdained the empty-calorie
consumption of what he saw on stage, 'the incredible, the
impossible, the superhuman...supplied by bombast, inflation,
and the piling of crimes on catastrophes and factitious raptures on
artificial agonies'. Instead, he says, theatre must provide 'heroes in
whom we can recognize our own humanity, and who, instead of
walking, talking, eating, drinking, sleeping, making love and
fighting single combats in a monotonous ecstasy of continuous
heroism, are heroic in the true human fashion: that is, touching
the summits only at rare moments'. Besides, Shaw believed, 'the
quality of a play is the quality of its ideas', and even the plays
which purported to seriously address real world issues of gender
and social class, to Shaw's dismay, were still flush with melodrama
and only provided superficial, reductive moral assessments of
characters and situations.

In 1898, he shared with *Saturday Review* readers that the
experience of undergoing a surgical procedure on his foot enabled
him finally to understand the 'British drama and the British actor'.
Awakening from a 'state of annihilation with ether', Shaw was
surprised that his 'character did not come back all at once', that his
'common sense [and] incorrigible Protestant respectability' were
preceded by the return of his 'sentimental side':

> For the first time in my life I tasted the bliss of having no morals to
> restrain me from lying, and no sense of reality to restrain me from
> romancing [as well as the opportunity] to prolong that condition
> indefinitely by taking a whiff or two of ether whenever I feel the
> chill of a moral or intellectual impulse. I can write plays in it;

I can act in it; I can gush in it: ... I can be pious and patriotic in it; I can melt touchingly over disease and death and murder and hunger and cold and poverty in it, turning all the woes of the world into artistic capital for myself.

Aiming to combat in his criticism and his journalism such an 'absolutely fictitious' state of public 'consciousness' in the theatre, in the media, and in the world, the quirky but sonorous voice of GBS sought to awaken audiences dangerously anaesthetized by vapid and trite romanticism.

On the page and in the streets, GBS seemed to be everywhere. An active walker, cyclist, and swimmer throughout most of his life, Shaw's busy-ness during his early years in London attracted notice and became quickly mythologized as proof of Shavian exceptionalism. In 1897, *The Vegetarian* reported that 'in the pursuit of his duties he has to work frequently under most unhealthy conditions and to face all weathers yet any observant stranger would turn and take a second look at Shaw's virile figure in the street'. Archibald Henderson, one of his early biographers, called him 'the quintessence of vital energy [who] rushes hither and thither, from one task to another, with a feverish, almost frenzied activity'. In fact, he fought as both a middleweight and a heavyweight in the Amateur Boxing Championships in March 1883 and vigorously pursued active hobbies that dovetailed with his interest in new technology, including photography, motoring, motorcycling, and air flight. Beneath his vibrant veneer, though, Shaw was always anxiously preoccupied with his health, particularly his crippling headaches, for which he would unsuccessfully search for medical, commercial, and homeopathic remedies his entire life. In the late 1890s, no longer able to sustain his delirious schedule, his health wholly collapsed, following a series of illnesses, injuries, and serious fluctuations in weight and appetite. With typical vim, he would later blame it on the moribund theatre, claiming that what had 'very nearly killed' him was repeatedly crossing the 'fatal threshold of a London playhouse', which had in turn caused his 'soul [to] become inane and [feed] unnaturally on his body'.

In his 21 May 1898 final contribution to the *Saturday Review*, Shaw reflected upon the toll his frenetic years of prolific personal and professional activity in London had taken but still nonetheless marvelled upon their accomplishment:

> Do I receive any spontaneous recognition for the prodigies of skill and industry I lavish on an unworthy institution and a stupid public? Not a bit of it: half my time is spent in telling people what a clever man I am. It is no use merely doing clever things in England. The English do not know what to think until they are coached, laboriously and insistently for years, in the proper and becoming opinion. For ten years past, with an unprecedented pertinacity and obstination, I have been dinning into the public head that I am an extraordinarily witty, brilliant, and clever man. That is now part of the public opinion of England; and no power in heaven or on earth will ever change it. I may dodder and dote; I may potboil and platitudinize; I may become the butt and chopping block of the bright, original spirits of the rising generation; but my reputation shall not suffer: it is built up fast and solid, like Shakespear's, on an impregnable basis of dogmatic reiteration.

Presaging the advent of modern celebrity branding, Shaw's boisterous self-promotion across multiple media platforms was eminently prosperous in forging GBS in the public's imagination.

Exhausted, he resigned in 1898 from the *Saturday Review*, effectively giving up his career as a critic to devote his energies full time to writing *for* the theatre rather than about it. Heightening his proficiency as a writer and providing a crucible for his blossoming political, metaphysical, and aesthetic views, the germination of GBS was crucial to Shaw's emerging dramaturgy as he had articulated in great detail his vision for stage reform in his critical writing: 'I postulated as desirable a certain kind of play in which I was destined ten years later to make my mark as a playwright...and I brought everybody, authors, actors, managers, to the one test: were they coming my way or staying in the old grooves?' Disappointed by the lack of traction generated by his critical exhortations, Shaw complains in his final review, titled 'Valedictory', that, rather than 'looking up to [him] as their guide, philosopher, and friend', theatre managers still regard him as 'the author of a series of weekly outrages on their profession and their privacy'. Undaunted, at the turn of the century, he pivots his primary focus to dramatic authorship as the prompt for creative evolution of British drama.

Shaw's abandonment of criticism does not in any way signify a detachment from the world; he had already begun in the early 1890s to write plays that, as he writes in *The Sanity of Art*, regardless of their setting, 'never study any period but the present'. His dramaturgy would always be animated by a journalist's sense of purpose—to expose hypocrisy, raise awareness, and facilitate sincere discussion about humanity's most urgent questions. And he would continue to supply a steady diet to a public hungry for more GBS—periodical contributions (usually in the form of letters to the editor), frequent public speaking engagements, and interviews in which he tirelessly debunks sentimentalized claptrap of various sorts and advocates on behalf of an often tragically uncritical public for a programme of relentless scrutiny of government, industry, and propaganda of all kinds. For him, 'in a living society every day is a day of judgment; and its recognition as such is not the end of all things but the beginning of a real civilization'.

Chapter 2
'Unpleasant'

In 1898, stung by censorship and frustrated by his inability to get his first three plays (*Widowers' Houses*, *The Philanderer*, and *Mrs Warren's Profession*) publicly staged in England, Shaw published them together in a volume titled *Plays Unpleasant*. As literary drama, they could do an end run around government authority, timid theatre managers, and actors confounded by the demands of his scripts. To further particularize these published editions, Shaw notoriously added verbose prefaces to most of the plays, sometimes even longer than the plays themselves, in which he would talk at length about their themes, staging possibilities, inspirations, satirical targets, and even topics only tenuously related to the play itself. On the page, he could have full control over the audience's experience as he did in his critical reviews, guide the interpretation of the play, and amplify its relationship to the world outside the theatre. Publication also afforded much stronger copyright protection for the author and gave him access to a wider reading audience to spur what he called 'serious advance' of the genre.

Underscoring his interest in the stage as a social weapon, he chose the title because the plays' 'dramatic power is used to force the spectator to face unpleasant facts':

> No doubt all plays which deal sincerely with humanity must wound the monstrous conceit which it is the business of romance to flatter.

But here we are confronted, not only with the comedy and tragedy
of individual character and destiny, but with those social horrors
which arise from the fact that the average homebred Englishman,
however honorable and goodnatured he may be in his private
capacity, is, as a citizen, a wretched creature who...will shut his
eyes to the most villainous abuses if the remedy threatens to add
another penny in the pound to the rates and taxes which he has to
be half cheated, half-coerced into paying.

His first play *Widowers' Houses* (1892) focuses on what its
author readily admits is 'not a pleasant theme' but one that
loomed large over his childhood experience in Dublin and was
inescapable in London: the shameful living conditions of
the working poor in urban slums. In its preface, he targets
'middle-class respectability and younger son gentility fattening
on the poverty of the slum as flies fatten on filth'. For Shaw,
playwriting was, like journalism, another opportunity to
confront a culture with its own moral hypocrisy and provoke
discussion of 'unmentionable' topics tied to discrimination,
injustice, and social oppression. *The Philanderer* (1893) and
Mrs Warren's Profession (1893) tackle the constrictions for
women in relation to money and marriage. Not a lurid or
shallow provocateur, Shaw's heterodoxy with regard to the
subject matter of his plays sought to unsettle and awaken his
audiences, hopefully inspiring them to support reform.

From the start, GBS was unapologetically 'unpleasant' as an
outspoken activist wanting to talk about what wasn't talked
about, and he unremittingly gave speeches, participated in
debates, and wrote pamphlets, newspaper op-eds, and magazine
pieces on behalf of public health reform, vegetarianism, and
political enfranchisement and against discrimination, animal
cruelty, and a socio-economic system predicated on a large
swathe of its inhabitants living in squalor. In 1933, his friend
Gilbert Murray summed up 'Shaw's business' as his friend
tirelessly working

to show something that was wrong and not known to be wrong; to throw a dazzling light upon it and, even by exaggeration and unfairness, to compel people to see something which they were unable or unwilling to see.

Charges of unpleasantness could hardly be avoided by someone who so fearlessly condemned structures of privilege, the hypocritical dogma that conspired to veil them, and those who shamefully benefited from them. In this sense, GBS's impertinence was a defining trait, proceeding from a devotion to querulously aggravating the established orthodoxies of popular thinking (Figure 3).

Two influences were key in Shaw's turn towards the British stage as another platform for his activism and specifically to his crafting of a new style of play, what he termed the 'drama of thought' that would illuminate and indict *systems* of oppression through staged discussion that eschewed the usual Victorian recrimination of individuals acting within those systems. Fortuitously in 1883, in the Reading Room of the British Museum, he met William Archer, who was among the first to translate Henrik Ibsen's plays into English so that they could circulate among readers prior to reaching the London stage. It was Archer's reading aloud from his own translation of *Peer Gynt* in 1888 that galvanized Shaw's interest in Ibsen, who gave him a narrative model that realized his view of the stage as a site for the dramatization of contemporary, 'unpleasant' social issues. Through translations, the Norwegian playwright grew to assume a considerable presence in the leftist circles Shaw ran in, and two dozen English productions of his plays in London occurred between 1889 and 1897, including Elizabeth Robins's landmark *Hedda Gabler* and a production of *Rosmersholm* with which Shaw was directly involved. All were not only influential on the fledgling playwright but instrumental in cementing a certain sensational reputation for Ibsen in England, and Shaw well knew the value of throwing himself into a controversy.

3. Shaw at 35 (1891).

The Quintessence of Ibsenism (1891)

In July 1890, Shaw delivered an extended lecture to the Fabian Society, the first section eventually forming the basis of his published study *The Quintessence of Ibsenism* in which he analysed in detail the playwright's body of work and articulated its dramaturgical vision. The other part of his talk used historical events and examples from Ibsen's plays to illustrate his contention that the cancerous idealism he observed in English Socialist thought was distracting the movement from its practical goals of social reform. *The Quintessence* sought to understand how it is 'that Ibsen, a Norwegian playwright of European celebrity, attracts one section of the English people so strongly that they hail him as the greatest living dramatic poet and moral teacher, whilst another section is so revolted by his works that they describe him in terms which they themselves admit are, by the necessities of the case, all but obscene.'

Rather than align himself with either the fanatical devotees or the equally rabid detractors, Shaw argues that both camps oversimplify the moral issues in Ibsen's plays because they view them 'through idealist spectacles'. The first three chapters of *The Quintessence* sketch his notion of Ibsen's vision of social progress, a process that is 'strewn with the wreckage of duties and ideals':

> Every new ideal is less of an illusion than the one it has supplanted; so that the destroyer of ideals, though denounced as an enemy of society, is in fact sweeping the world clear of lies.

Close readings of twelve of Ibsen's plays make the case that Ibsen, for Shaw, 'repudiates duties, tramples on ideals, profanes what was sacred, sanctifies what was infamous, always driving his plough through gardens of pretty weeds'. *The Quintessence* situates Ibsen within a tradition of reform anchored by Percy Bysshe Shelley, one that also was crucial in the formulation of the 'GBS' persona and eventually the lens through which Shaw approached his own writing for the theatre.

Throughout *The Quintessence*, Shaw reaffirms that Ibsen's plays deserve their reputation of 'immoral tendency' only as it has to do with representing 'conduct, mischievous or not, which does not conform to current ideals', and his own first three plays would garner the same charges. In 1882, Archer wrote that 'a drama which opens the slightest intellectual, moral, or political question is certain to fail. The public will accept open vice, but it will have nothing to do with...a piece to whose theme the word "unpleasant" can be applied.' Shaw, of course, chose that word as the title of his first volume of published plays, and doing so was his declaration of a manifesto, of how he understood the mission of the stage in relation to its social context. He maintained that 'fine art is the subtlest, the most seductive, the most effective instrument of moral propaganda in the world':

> The art of the stage...works by exhibiting examples of personal conduct made intelligible and moving to crowds of unobservant unreflecting people...and so effective do I find the dramatic method that I have no doubt I shall at last persuade even London to take its conscience and its brains with it when it goes to the theatre.

Widowers' Houses (1892)

Inspired by Ibsen, Shaw composed his first three plays in distinctive keys but all to illustrate that 'the idealist is a more dangerous animal than a Philistine just as a man is a more dangerous animal than a sheep'. What would become his very first, *Widowers' Houses*, began as an 1884 collaboration with him providing the dialogue and Archer the plot. Though he eagerly started writing, Shaw quickly abandoned the task when he could find nothing worth doing with the fashionable 'twaddling cup-and-saucer comedy' scenario given to him by his friend. J. T. Grein's infamous 1891 production of Ibsen's *Ghosts* propelled

Shaw back to the unfinished play, determined this time not to adhere to hackneyed stage precepts but to appropriate them in the service of a different dramaturgical goal. When he finished it in 1892, Ibsen's influence is clear, but the play is individuated already with what would become innovative staples of Shavian drama, including the greying of melodrama's black/white morality, the inclusion of an extended discussion scene, and an ending that eschewed conventional closure. Shaw hoped that the swelling interest in staging Ibsen's plays might spill over into performance possibilities for *Widowers' Houses*, which was, according to its subtitle, a 'Didactic Reality Play'. Unfortunately, although it was first produced privately in December 1892, it would not receive its first public staging for another fifteen years.

While evasive in providing a solution to the problem it uncovers, the play's tactic is typically Shavian; rather than demonize those individual characters who feed upon slum revenue, the playwright seeks to expose the hypocrisy of a society that not only allows such poverty but economically depends upon it. The impact of sordid social inequality upon Shaw, which he witnessed in both Dublin and London, was profound. Between 1897 and 1903, he served as a vestryman and worked actively with the local Health Committee on community hygiene issues. As biographer Michael Holroyd notes, he 'visited workhouses, hospitals, sweatshops and the homes of the poor and saw destitution and disease. Many of the tenements were lice-ridden; there were epidemics of smallpox, and occasional cases of typhoid fever, and even bubonic plague.' That experience surely fuelled his commitment to eradicate impoverishment through the elimination of substandard living and working conditions and the implementation of a nationalized health service, but its horror reverberates throughout his entire body of writing and animates his earliest play, although viewed from the top down rather than from the ground up.

Widowers' Houses begins typically enough for a romantic comedy when, on holiday in Germany, Dr Harry Trench meets and wishes to marry Blanche Sartorius. The tone of the play shifts when, back in London, Trench shockingly discovers slum profiteering as the source of his intended's family income and begs her to renounce her inheritance, only to be shown by her father how his own money is derived from the same source. The play's final act takes place four months later when Blanche herself finds out the secret and aggressively woos Trench back to form a profitable alliance in a new scheme involving the shrewd resale of such properties to the government. Shaw recasts the standard comic formula of boy and girl striving to overcome a parental barrier to their nuptials with the help of a clever servant (in this case, Sartorius' former rent-collector Lickcheese) as a lesson in economics via a dramatized portrait of human depravity and collusion. As he wrote later in a letter to Archer:

> Why did I write it? ... Because I wanted to show up the slums and the cash nexus between them and the squares.

Despite its only receiving two private performances in December of 1892 by Grein's Independent Theatre Society, *Widowers' Houses* still caused a critical flap, due partly to its content but also to its unusual style. *The Speaker*'s A. B. Walkley, for instance, called it a 'bad play' despite its 'considerable literary qualities' because 'Shaw's people are not dramatic characters at all, they are embodied arguments', a view that would dog the perception of Shaw's dramaturgy throughout his career. Perhaps as much drawn to the furore created as to the political possibilities of the drama, though, Shaw decided to keep writing.

The Philanderer (1893)

The second *Unpleasant* play, the much-revised comedy *The Philanderer*, in part grew from Shaw's extensive romantic escapades in London and in part from his experiences in the city's leftist intellectual culture. The plot concerns a day in the life of Leonard Charteris as he encourages amorous attention from but discourages commitment with two different women. As he was writing it, Shaw began an affair with the actress Florence Farr without fully having extricated himself from his previous relationship with another woman called Jenny Patterson. When, in February of 1893, Patterson stormed into Farr's apartment and caught the two together, the intense and awkward situation that resulted eventually was reworked into the play's opening scene.

Shaw called it a 'Topical Comedy', and indeed it was, replete with many references to current political and social questions as well as subjects that chronically riled Shaw, such as animal vivisection, quack medicine, convoluted divorce laws, and even the absurd dictates of conventional comedy. In conception, *The Philanderer* is grounded much more firmly in autobiography than its predecessor, reflecting in its London setting the avant-garde milieu within which Shaw built his early reputation. In that sense, it was almost too contemporary, and Shaw had difficulty finding a theatre willing to take a risk producing a play deemed by one rejection note 'vulgar and immoral and cynically disrespectful to ladies and gentlemen'. Finished in 1893, it would not receive its first full production—besides the staged reading arranged by Shaw in 1898 in order to secure his copyright—until 1907.

The Philanderer goes after Victorian ideals with a vengeance, especially with regard to marriage and stifling conceptions of middle-class femininity. The ideal wife was encouraged to self-efface and place herself solely in the service of her husband, and, legally, she was his property, which, to Fabian socialists, was just another instance of economic subjugation. As such, they championed the creation of expanded educational and professional opportunities for women and supported their enfranchisement. In the 1890s, the term 'New Woman' denoted those who were pushing back against the constrictions of traditional gender roles and asserting intellectual, emotional, financial, and sexual autonomy. A proponent of simple divorce arrangements and economic equality, Shaw maintained that 'unless Woman repudiates her womanliness, her duty to her husband, to her children, to society, to the law, and to everyone but herself, she cannot emancipate herself'. Such statements—sounding a bit like those Nora Helmer makes at the end of *A Doll's House*—again reflect Ibsen's deep influence politically and dramaturgically on the novice playwright.

Setting its second act in the 'Ibsen Club', *The Philanderer* is chock full of both 'unwomanly women' and 'unmanly men', but Shaw's young characters are not earnest cardboard poster children for social change but full embodiments of the confusions, infirmities, and contradictions not only of rapid cultural change but of early adulthood, under the spell of ego, hormones, and urban freedom. He is able to spoof the conservative anxieties surrounding the Ibsenist prospect of female equality while at the same time critiquing the superficial parroting of Ibsen's ideas, trendy within a certain urban progressive community. Originally, Shaw conceived and wrote a third act to *The Philanderer* that curiously departed in style from the rest of the play, including more extended focus on critiquing divorce law and the medical profession. He ultimately discarded it, writing in his diary that it 'started on quite a new trail', in favour of a new ending that both confirms and diverges from audience expectations. Shaw twists the 'happily ever after' closure of traditional comedy with a marriage evaporated of sexual desire and romantic love, unexorcized from the spectre of future philandering.

Some material from the abandoned act would be recycled later in *The Doctor's Dilemma* (1906), a tragedy that explores professional ethics among a group of doctors. The dilemma occurs when Dr Ridgeon must choose between saving the life of the artist Louis Dubedat, equal parts charm and scoundrel, and that of colleague Dr Blenkinsop, an impoverished and flawed general practitioner. Complementing the play's satire is a preface that lodges a full frontal assault on the moral infirmities of practitioners, medical science, and especially vivisection, the cruelty of which had been a focus of Shaw's ire since the late 1880s. Shaw was also unconvinced by germ theory and suspicious of the efficacy of vaccination, stemming from his own experience in 1881 when he contracted smallpox despite having been inoculated against it. (His trademark beard may actually have first been cultivated to hide the resulting scars.) Shaw frequently railed against the false claims of the patent medicine industry, the criminal inadequacy of public health service, and treatment protocol predicated on animal experimentation and profuse with unnecessary surgeries, incompetence, and outright fraud. As it was for his fellow Fabians, though, the real villain was the economic system for condemning a large section of the population to malnourishment, abject poverty, and no access to proper sanitation.

Other content cast off from *The Philanderer* would seed a later comedy called *Getting Married* (1908) in which guests, gathered for the nuptials of Edith Bridgenorth and Cecil Sykes, lament the disappointments, unfairness, and cruelties of being in a marriage as well as the legal difficulty of getting out of one. They go on to consider a range of prospective responses to the infirmities of the institution, including celibacy, philandering, and separatism. As he writes in the play's preface, 'marriage remains practically inevitable; and the sooner we acknowledge this, the sooner we shall set to work to make it decent and reasonable'. Written without act or scene breaks, *Getting Married* is a paradigmatic example of a Shavian hallmark, what its subtitle calls the 'disquisitory play'. In a 1908 interview with the *Daily Telegraph*, Shaw illuminated his rationale for *Getting Married*:

> If you look at any of the old editions of our classical plays, you will see that the description of the play is not called a plot or a story, but an argument. That exactly describes the material of my play. It is an argument—an argument lasting nearly three hours and carried on with unflagging cerebration by twelve people and a beadle.

Returning to plays of this kind over and over throughout his career, up to *The Apple Cart* (1929) and *In Good King Charles's*

Golden Days (1939), Shaw believed that discussion should form the essence of drama, and he understood conversation *as* action with more conventional story tropes relegated to the background, functioning solely as an occasion for meaningful talk. His skill at crafting eloquent, riveting, and explosive stage dialogue though is abundantly evident even in these first plays and reaches an early summit in the two extended powerhouse exchanges between a mother and daughter that form the core of Shaw's third *Unpleasant* play.

Mrs Warren's Profession (1893)

Mrs Warren's Profession concerns two generations of women squaring off over their very different life choices and values and concludes, like Ibsen's *A Doll's House*, with a mother slamming an exit door. Kitty Warren is Nora Helmer's contemporary who has not married but has achieved enough entrepreneurial success on her own to provide a very expensive education for her daughter Vivie. Smart, articulate, and direct, Vivie likes whiskey, cigars, and detective novels and is bored by classical music and the National Gallery. Loathing vacations in the country, she nevertheless has come to a cottage in Surrey at the start of the play to see her mother, about whom she knows very little and with whom she expects to engage in a 'battle royal' over her professional ambitions to establish an office in London and make a living at actuarial calculation.

Like *Widowers' Houses*, *Mrs Warren's Profession* turns upon the discovery of tainted money; in this case, Kitty's proficiency at running an international chain of brothels at first causes Vivie to recoil in moral horror. At her mother's wish to explain the circumstances that lead to her partnership with her sister in the venture, Vivie is unreceptive:

> People are always blaming their circumstances for what they are. I don't believe in circumstances. The people who get on in this world

are the people who get up and look for the circumstances they want, and if they can't find them, make them.

Kitty chastises her daughter's 'easy talk' and goes on to relate how she saw her half-sisters play by the rules only to meet gruesome fates, one enduring twelve-hour workdays in a paint factory only to die of lead poisoning and the other a poverty-stricken mother of three married to an alcoholic. Kitty asks Vivie: 'How could you keep your self-respect in such starvation and slavery? And what's a woman worth? What's life worth? Without self-respect?' In *The Quintessence of Ibsenism*, Shaw had written in a similar vein:

> Our society, being directly dominated by men, comes to regard Woman, not as an end in herself like Man, but solely as a means of ministering to his appetite....To treat a person as a means instead of an end is to deny that person's right to life....Woman, if she dares face the fact that she is being so treated, must either loathe herself or else rebel.

Following her mother's disclosure, Vivie is in awe: 'My dear mother: you are a wonderful woman: you are stronger than all England.' Both women commiserate over societal iniquity but vouch for practicality:

> It can't be right, Vivie, that there shouldn't be better opportunities for women. I stick to that: it's wrong. But it's so, right or wrong; and a girl must make the best of it.

Kitty's investor and friend George Crofts puts it more crassly to Vivie late in the play: 'While we're in this world, we're in it; and money's money.'

Their reconciliation unfortunately is short-lived, once Vivie finds out that her mother has continued in her profession long after it has made her enough to live on comfortably and long after her sister has retired. Condemning Kitty and refusing any more of her money, she flees to London and sets up shop with her mentor, Honoria Fraser. In the final scene, Vivie is visited there by the aesthete Praed and rejects his offer of a trip to Italy, repudiating what he calls the 'Gospel of Art' in favour of the 'Gospel of Getting On'. The 'cleverly good-for-nothing' Frank Gardner also circles her throughout the play with matrimonial ambitions but eventually withdraws when it is clear that Vivie will disavow her inheritance. If her relationship to either of the men is to continue any further in the future, she demands to be 'treated as a woman of business, permanently single and permanently unromantic'. Vivie gets one last visit from her mother who is stunned that her daughter is throwing away a life of privilege and wealth to be a 'mere drudge, toiling and moiling early and late for your bare living and two cheap dresses a year':

> You're throwing away all your chances for nothing. You think people are what they pretend to be: that the way you were taught at school and college to think right and proper is the way things really are. But it's not: it's all only a pretence, to keep the cowardly slavish common run of people quiet.

Vivie counters:

> I know very well that fashionable morality is all a pretence, and that if I took your money and devoted the rest of my life to spending it fashionably, I might be as worthless and vicious as the silliest woman could possibly want to be without having a word said to me about it. But I don't want to be worthless.

Preferring to take life 'as it is', Vivie also objects to Kitty's sentimentality and adherence to tenets of middle-class morality such as duty and respectability, her steadfast determination 'to live one life but believe in another'. Refusing her daughter's request to shake hands, the upset Kitty storms out, and the play ends with Vivie at her desk 'absorbed in [the work's] figures'.

As he did in his first play, Shaw avoids the position on the issue taken by Victorian moralists who ascribe degeneracy to the prostitutes themselves and instead exposes a systemic vision of economic disenfranchisement, exploitation, and hypocrisy. With his unapologetic and bold Kitty, he rebukes the 'fallen woman' character type, very popular on the late 19th-century stage, whose 'proper' punishment for her past transgressions for Shaw obscured the real shame and squalor of the trade's very existence. The very first sentence of his preface reads: 'Prostitution is caused not by female depravity and male licentiousness, but simply by underpaying, undervaluing, and overworking women so shamefully that the poorest of them are forced to resort to prostitution to keep body and soul together.' In short, as he would later write, the 'root of the evil is economic', and thus he draws Kitty sympathetically, strongly differentiating her from her 'fallen' counterparts in other contemporary plays. As scholar L. W. Conolly asserts,

> Mrs. Warren is not a repentant prostitute, nor by the end of the play is she a *dead* prostitute. Far from it. At the end of the play she is bruised by her daughter's rejection, but otherwise she is alive and well and looking forward to managing her brothels enthusiastically, efficiently, and indefinitely.

A play 'written for women', *Mrs Warren's Profession*, like *Widowers' Houses*, brings injustice to the light by widening the lens on the problem to demonstrate, in this case, how the profits of the industry are not simply hoarded by the brothel owners themselves but, in Shaw's words,

> by the landlords of their houses, the newspapers which advertise them, the restaurants which cater for them, and, in short, all the trades to which they are good customers, not to mention the public officials and representatives whom they silence by complicity, corruption, or blackmail. Add to these the employers who profit by cheap female labor, and the shareholders whose dividends depend

on it (you find such people everywhere, even on the judicial bench and in the highest places in Church and State), and you get a large and powerful class with a strong pecuniary incentive to protect Mrs Warren's profession, and a correspondingly strong incentive to conceal, from their own consciences no less than from the world, the real sources of their gain.

Kitty's remark in the play that 'the only way for a woman to provide for herself decently is for her to be good to some man that can afford to be good to her' further expands the traffic in women to include by implication marriage as a kind of de facto prostitution. Remarkable in political vision but grounded in the complex and shifting relationships of fully humanized characters, *Mrs Warren's Profession* is the play in which Shaw really *arrives* as a serious playwright, compellingly staging the discussion of ideas and urgent social issues he so valued to deliver both intellectual *and* emotional punches.

As before, though, Shaw encountered problems over *Mrs Warren's Profession*'s 'unpleasant' subject matter. Since the 18th century, playwrights in England were required to submit all new works to the Examiner of Plays, a government official given the authority to license plays for performance only if he deemed them appropriate for public consumption. The office had been created as a watchdog for seditious propaganda but was loosely defined enough to facilitate the banning of plays that contained any direct questioning or critiques of state or religious authority or any content that challenged the decorum of polite society. With *Mrs Warren's Profession*, even in order to receive authorization for a single private performance to establish copyright, Shaw was forced to revise what most troubled the Examiner, namely Mrs Warren's profession, to that of a pickpocket. The play would not receive its first full production until January 1902 under the auspices of the Stage Society, an independent group founded by a fellow Fabian and, as a private club, beyond the reach of the Examiner of Plays. Even this modest presentation was vexatious for the critics. *The Sunday Special* described an 'exceedingly uncomfortable afternoon' in which Shaw 'has merely philandered around a dangerous subject' and decried as 'unnecessary and painful...a play of a needlessly unpleasant understructure to no useful end'.

If *Widowers' Houses* had created a stir, *Mrs Warren's Profession* provoked an absolute uproar when it crossed the Atlantic in 1905. Following a raucous opening night in New Haven, Connecticut, the mayor shut down all further performances in response to calls from irate constituents and indignant reviews in the local papers, including the *New Haven Leader*, which pronounced it 'the most shockingly immoral dialogue ever publicly repeated'. The production moved to New York and opened three days later at the Garrick Theatre, and its second public showing (replete with a slightly revised script) engendered an even more dramatic reaction. Crowds swarmed the streets surrounding the theatre hoping to get a ticket, with thousands turned away when every seat was quickly filled. The following day, outrage surged through the press notices, typified by the *New York Herald*'s charge that the 'morally rotten' play 'defends immorality, glorifies debauchery, [and] countenances the most revolting form of degeneracy'. In due course, the city's police commissioner informed the theatre's manager that no subsequent performances were permitted and that the company would be arrested on a charge of 'offending public decency'. Shaw commented to the American periodical *The Sun* that the fuss was exactly what the play was getting at in that

> it will be seen more and more clearly that the police, doubtless with the best intentions, are protecting not public morality but the interest of the most dangerous class, namely, the employers who pay women less than subsistence wages and overwork them mercilessly to grind profits for themselves out of the pith of the nation.

After a series of delays caused by surging crowds in front of the courthouse and aggressive paparazzi attempting to get photographs and interviews, the charges would eventually be dropped in July 1906. The controversy perfectly illustrated one of the playwright's 'Maxims for Revolutionists': 'Decency is Indecency's conspiracy of silence.'

While Shaw claimed in the preface to *Mrs Warren's Profession* that he 'could not have done anything more injurious to [his] prospects at the outset of [his] career' than to write such a polarizing drama, his 'unpleasant' plays solidified the precise reputation he was after:

> I am not an ordinary playwright....I am a specialist in immoral and heretical plays. My reputation has been gained by my persistent struggle to force the public to reconsider its morals.

As such, he counts himself among what he termed the Diabolists, alongside Friedrich Nietzsche, Richard Wagner, and of course Henrik Ibsen, who put established doctrines in quotation marks and subjected them to scrupulous examination, devil's disciples all.

Despite Shaw's ongoing attempts to get the play licensed, *Mrs Warren's Profession* would not be given a full public production in England until 1925, when he 'once again shared with Ibsen the triumphant amusement of startling all but the strongest-headed of the London theatre critics clean out of the practice of their profession'. According to *The Quintessence of Ibsenism*, 'the plain working truth is that it is not only good for people to be shocked occasionally but absolutely necessary to the progress of society that they should be shocked pretty often'. Shaw's first three plays show his understanding of the stage as providing a unique opportunity for Fabian activism, for not only exposing social issues but for challenging the audience's unexamined assumptions about and complicities with a system that urgently needs reform. One of *Mrs Warren's* characters points out that, 'as long as you don't fly openly in the face of society, society doesn't ask any inconvenient questions'. As a writer, Shaw's ethos was to be the one openly asking (and usually answering) inconvenient questions; however, if he was going to reach the public stage, he realized he needed to adjust his dramaturgy in order to bypass demoralizing and paralysing collisions with the Examiner's office.

Chapter 3
'Pleasant'

If his subject matter was often 'unpleasant', Shaw's rhetorical style paradoxically was quite the opposite. As biographer A. M. Gibbs puts it,

> as a born controversialist and iconoclast, his intellectual stance was frequently pugnacious and antagonistic. His tone and manner, by contrast, were generally courteous, amusing, and disarming.

An amiable and often cheerful agitator, GBS was charming and funny during speeches and in debates, and his savage brandishing of irony and jokes as well as his affinity for exaggeration and showmanship were essential in distinguishing his voice on the page and on the platform from those of his competitors and opponents in London during the 1880s and 1890s (Figure 4). In the 17th century, according to the *Oxford English Dictionary*, the word 'pleasant' was a noun that referred to 'a jester, a clown, a fool'. But Shaw was not interested in humour for humour's sake. While he felt that 'irresponsible laughter is salutary in small quantities', much more meaningful was *responsible* laughter, that is to say, comedy with an agenda. In 1898, he published a companion volume to *Plays Unpleasant* titled *Plays Pleasant*, containing *Arms and the Man* (1893–4), *Candida* (1894), *The Man of Destiny* (1895), and *You Never Can Tell* (1895–6). These, Shaw maintained, were responses to 'requests from West End

4. GBS clowning.

theatres for fashionable comedies' that satisfied the 'popular
preference for fun' without sacrificing their critical faculties. From
these initial forays in the genre to late plays like *The Millionairess*
(1935) and *Buoyant Billions* (1946), Shaw turned tropes drawn
from romantic and sentimental comedy, the comedy of manners,

and even farce against one another. Rather than cater to the audience's assumptions and expectations, Shaw sought to revise them; for him, as he wrote in 1897, comedy's endgame 'is nothing less than the destruction of old-established morals'.

Frequently making characters who adhere to conventional values and beliefs buffoonish, Shaw wielded what he called 'the fierce castigation of comedy and the ruthless light of laughter' as part of his efforts to reclaim the theatre as an arena dedicated to the exchange of ideas, the exploration of the human condition, and the dissection of the status quo. To enable this transformation, he first had to get his plays on the stage, and his disarming talent to amuse proved his most valuable tool in doing so. While Shaw often downplayed the novelty of his dramaturgy, preferring to see it as simply 'an unaccustomed method of tickling' the world, playwright Bertolt Brecht was much more direct:

> The bomb he puts under the British class system is comedy, and
> the fuse is his frustration. It should be clear by now that Shaw is a
> terrorist. The Shavian terror is an unusual one, and he employs
> an unusual weapon—humour.

Arms and the Man (1893–4)

Fed up with the seeming futility of getting his 'unpleasant' dramas publicly produced, Shaw changed course from writing plays that directly attacked 'the crimes of society' to those that lampooned 'its romantic follies'—and his first, written the same year as *Mrs Warren's Profession*, was an attempt to translate his anti-idealism into the idiom of light comedy. *Arms and the Man* begins when a fleeing Serbian soldier named Bluntschli trespasses into the bedroom of Raina Petkoff, a naive young Bulgarian woman, and demands her protection. After hiding him from the search party, Raina is surprised to find him carrying an empty gun and chocolate creams as she listens to his account of the less than heroic exploits of her fiancé Sergius Saranoff, a cavalry officer in the Bulgarian army. The following year, Sergius and Raina's father return from the war, still smarting over being outwitted by Bluntschli, who soon after also returns to the Petkoff household to give back a coat lent to him as a disguise during his escape. Sergius, despite his matrimonial engagement and perhaps wearied by Raina's high-minded talk of the nobility of love, is drawn instead to Louka, an assertive servant, yet nonetheless challenges Bluntschli to a duel. Shaw concludes the comedy with two couplings, Raina/Bluntschli and Louka/Sergius, that each twist audience expectations. Through all of the near-farcical goings on, Bluntschli deflates Raina's 'noble sentiment' about war even as the journey of the play for Sergius, like that of so many of Ibsen's characters, is also one of disillusionment. Careful to craft him, as he says, to be 'ridiculous through the breakdown of his ideals, not odious from his falling short of them', Shaw saw Sergius as a 'movingly human figure whose tragi-comedy is the true theme of the play'.

Arms and the Man was Shaw's first foray into the commercial theatre, the first of his plays to be seen in America, and the first to be made into a feature film (in 1932). Like the young Shakespeare, Shaw was very adept at writing comedy from the start, but *Arms and the Man*'s success gave him pause. Following the curtain call at the April 1894 opening, Shaw stepped on stage in response to repeated audience calls for the author; supposedly, amid rapturous applause arose a single loud 'Boo!', to which the playwright replied: 'My dear fellow, I quite agree with you. But what are we two against so many?' While its popularity would bring to him his first fiscal rewards as a playwright, Shaw struggled with what his shift to pleasantness might cost in relation to his social and theatrical reform agenda. He originally subtitled *Arms and the Man* 'a romantic comedy' but, worried that the potent humour distracted audience members from his earnest thematic intent, later changed it to 'an anti-romantic comedy'. He wanted theatregoers to approach the genre not as a carnival for mindless pleasure but as a laboratory for mindful enquiry. As he had written in the *Saturday Review*, 'the function of comedy is to dispel...unconsciousness by turning the searchlight of the keenest moral and intellectual analysis right on to it'. Yet, the right balance was tricky to achieve, as he revealed in a 1928 speech to the Royal Academy of Dramatic Arts:

> Just when I am really rising to the height of my power that I may become really tragic and great, some absurd joke occurs and the anti-climax is irresistible....I cannot deny that I've got the tragedian and I have got the clown in me; and the clown trips me up in the most dreadful way.

Candida (1894)

Another *Pleasant* play titled *Candida* makes clear that Shaw was not simply Anglicizing Ibsen but actively in dialogue with his illustrious predecessor. In it, a young poet called Eugene Marchbanks declares his love for Candida Morell and denounces her marriage to the Reverend James Morell on the grounds that her husband does not understand her and that he is beneath her. At first upset at the boy's arrogance in calling him a 'moralist and a windbag', Morell is further stunned when Candida disillusions him that his sermons are successful only because his female parishioners have crushes on him, not because they subscribe to his Christian Socialist principles. In the meantime, Candida seriously ponders her responsibilities in relation to the needs of both men, especially fearful what will happen to his art if Marchbanks in his search for inspiration should fall in with wayward women. After extended discussion, Candida, by turns nurturing and aggressive, reveals that her final choice is to minister to 'the weaker of the two', James:

> I build a castle of comfort and indulgence and love for him, and stand sentinel always to keep little vulgar cares out. I make him master here, though he does not know it.

The play's conclusion is marked by yet another angrily slammed door, as the defeated Marchbanks departs; Shaw would state much later on that *Candida* was 'a counterblast to Ibsen's *A Doll's House*, showing that in the real typical doll's house it is the man who is the doll'.

Even so, Candida's 'choice' is to play one of two defined patriarchal roles for women, the muse or the angel-in-the-house, so, as much authority as she wields within the household, her identity is still circumscribed by repressive gender ideology. In contrast to Nora Helmer storming out at the conclusion of *A Doll's House*, Candida stays put, and *Candida* risks validating in its conventional ending what it purports to interrogate. Aghast that its initial audiences were reduced to tears at the final curtain and detesting such corruptive sentimentality, Shaw would later write against what he termed the 'Candidamaniacs' who set aside the character's pragmatic anti-idealism in favour of her hyper-maternal steadfastness. The novice dramatist was still navigating his shift from the provocative 'Unpleasant' didacticism to the tactical subterfuge of comic style demanded by 'Pleasant' theatre managers and audiences. Nonetheless, the play would eventually be key to establishing Shaw's reputation as an up and coming British playwright. *Candida*'s first public performance in London in 1904 would be part of the opening season of a repertory experiment at the Royal Court Theatre to showcase innovations in dramaturgy and theatrical practice. Across, the Atlantic, the 1903–4 New York production of *Candida* was crowned by *The New York Times* as 'the most talked-of event' of the season and set off in the city what the *New York Herald* called 'Bernard Shaw fever'.

You Never Can Tell (1895–6)

Following the stage success of *Arms and the Man*, Shaw was besieged by requests for similar plays that catered to the public's hunger for, as he described it, 'fashionable dresses, a little music, and even an exhibition of eating and drinking by people with an expensive air, attended by an if-possible comic waiter', all dramaturgical elements against which as critic he had frequently railed as corrosive to the art form. With *You Never Can Tell*, his intention was to show how, putting them to a purpose, 'the drama can humanize those things as easily as they, in the wrong hands, can dehumanize the drama'. Set at a seaside resort in southern England and occasioned by a chance encounter with a dentist, *You Never Can Tell* resembles *The Philanderer* in blending elements of farce with those of contemporary romantic comedy. When rehearsals began in 1897 for the premiere, though, the production soon fell apart when actors, baffled by the play's non-naturalistic tone, could not figure out how to play the roles. Max Beerbohm, the critic for the *Saturday Review*, agreed:

> It is rather difficult to figure out how [*You Never Can Tell*] ought to be acted. Realism and sheer fantasy are inexplicably entangled in the scheme of the play.

Expressed in his theatrical criticism as well as throughout his correspondence with theatre practitioners, Shaw's views on the craft of acting placed significant emphasis on voice, breath, and diction, which, at the dawn of naturalism, put him at odds with current inward-looking performance theory and practice. As a result, as with so many of Shaw's early plays, *You Never Can Tell*'s premiere in 1899 was just a single, private performance; its runaway success would have to wait until the spring of 1905.

The play begins just after a tooth extraction performed by Valentine on a young, energetic girl named Dolly Clandon. When the patient's family arrives, the rookie dentist falls in love at first sight with Dolly's older sister Gloria and receives an invitation to lunch with them. The meal is awkward due to the presence of

Valentine's prickly landlord Fergus Crampton who turns out to be the estranged father of the Clandon children. Valentine pursues Gloria, who is disappointed that she enjoys his kiss because she has been raised by her mother to be a New Woman. She is further aggravated to discover that Valentine is a philanderer but finds her personal will trumped by her romantic feelings:

> I am one of those weak creatures born to be mastered by the first man
> whose eye is caught by them; and I must fulfill my destiny, I suppose.

You Never Can Tell culminates in a fancy dress ball as Crampton works without certainty of success towards reconciliation with his ex-wife and Valentine, with Gloria in pursuit, prophesies that his days of bachelorhood may finally be numbered.

Like *Mrs Warren's Profession*, *You Never Can Tell* is a play that places at its centre a mother and daughter. Mrs. Clandon has left her abusive, alcoholic husband, raised her three children independently, and become a well-known writer of tracts with 'advanced ideas'. Moulded in her mother's image, Gloria nonetheless finds her intellect and individualist spirit no match for her emotions. But, while Gloria feels subdued, the power dynamic within the relationship clearly favours her, and she orders Valentine at the end of the play to

> get up. (*Valentine gets up abjectly.*) Now let us have no false delicacy.
> Tell my mother we have agreed to marry one another.

In response, the waiter remarks to Valentine:

> Every man is frightened of marriage when it comes to the point... *I* never was master in my own house, sir: my wife was like our young lady: she was of a commanding and masterful disposition.

Like traditional comedy, the play concludes with a young marriage but arranged in a decidedly unconventional hierarchy; the female may be subject to providence and to passion but not to her husband.

Even so, for all its 'pleasant' comedy, *You Never Can Tell*'s journey exacts costs from both women. Mrs. Clandon seems unable to ever reconcile with her husband while Gloria must come to terms with the limits of her personal autonomy, 'shocked, offended, horrified' and

> driven almost mad with shame by the feeling that all her power over herself had broken down at her first real encounter with— with—[*The color rushes over her face again.*]

The experience will become a rite of passage for many future Shaw characters, male and female, subordinated by a cosmic decree only vaguely sketched in this play, which they perceive as emotion but actually is a determined force working through them to stimulate evolutionary growth. For a playwright known for his commitment to rational analysis as the avenue to reform, *You Never Can Tell* expresses an openness to other powers in the universe and in the human heart that are comparably influential and often triumphant. In an 1896 letter to the actress Ellen Terry, Shaw wrote that 'man's one gift is that at his best he *can* love—not constantly, nor faithfully, nor often, nor for that long, but for a moment'. Shaw will soon develop further this conceit of a young man and woman yoked together by an irresistible universal drive in one of his masterpieces, *Man and Superman*.

Pygmalion (1912)

The zenith of Shaw's 'pleasant' comedy is undoubtedly *Pygmalion*, his most famous and beloved play. During the Edwardian period, the women's suffrage movement was at odds with itself about how best to further its cause, whether through reasoned public debate or through mass demonstration and civil protest. Since the early 1890s, Shaw had been an ally as both a speaker and author, challenging traditional patriarchal mythologies in his plays, speeches, essays, and other various public writings. Through this lens, *Pygmalion* is a play about emancipation that examines the challenges posed to self-determination by oppressive class and gender ideologies, especially as they inflect language. It begins with an unlikely Covent Garden encounter between a strong-willed Cockney flower-girl called Eliza Doolittle and an eccentric linguist incensed at her 'crooning like a bilious pigeon'. A professor of phonetics, Henry Higgins chastises her dialect as producing 'depressing and disgusting sounds' that belie her 'divine gift of articulate speech [and] native language [that] is the language of Shakespear and Milton'. He announces that he can purge her in three months of 'her kerbstone English, the English that will keep her in the gutter to the end of her days'. Such an experiment will demonstrate that caste differences are constructed, not natural, and that reforming language can bridge the imposed social distance between people. According to the play's preface, Shaw drew Higgins as an example of 'the reformer we need most today'; such 'an energetic phonetic enthusiast' can reclaim the spoken word from its class inflection and rebuild the culture more equitably, ultimately eliminating that plane of social existence in which you 'work til you are more a brute than a human being; and then cuddle and squabble and drink til you fall asleep'. The utopian dimensions to Higgins's project become clear when he later shares with Eliza that the 'great secret' is

> not having bad manners or good manners or any other particular
> sort of manners, but having the same manner for all human souls:
> in short, behaving as if you were in heaven, where there are no
> third-class carriages, and one soul is as good as another.

When Eliza shows up at Higgins's flat the following day, wishing to pay him for speech lessons, his roommate Colonel Pickering challenges him to pass her off as a duchess at the Ambassador's upcoming garden party, a wager he enthusiastically accepts. A second status transformation occurs in the play when Eliza's father Alfred unexpectedly inherits an enormous annual income that obligates him to don the constraining collar of middle-class morality. His experience echoes what eventually happens with Eliza as Shaw makes the point that mere social elevation of individuals is inadequate reform if the system itself remains unchanged.

After some intense sessions of diction instruction, Higgins brings the 'new' Eliza, reinvented if still a bit awkward in her new persona, to a social gathering given by his mother. Eliza's grammatical and syntactical slips do not deter the younger guests, Freddy and Clara Eynsford-Hill, from being fascinated. When she learns of the experiment, Mrs. Higgins pointedly enquires into Eliza's future, about which Higgins and Pickering seem unconcerned. Instead, Higgins smugly basks in the glow of professional accomplishment, the creation of what he calls 'a tower of strength: a consort battleship' from 'this thing out of the squashed cabbage leaves of Covent Garden'. Belonging in neither her old or new worlds, Eliza at last angrily revolts against what she considers their tyrannical lack of consideration for her feelings and well-being:

> Oh! If only I *could* go back to my flower basket! I should be independent of both you and father and all the world! Why did you take my independence from me? Why did I give it up? I'm a slave now, for all my fine clothes....You know very well all the time that you're nothing but a bully. You know I can't go back to the gutter, as you call it, and that I have no real friends in the world but you and Colonel Pickering.

For all of his reformist zeal, Higgins is genuinely disdainful of human beings, excepting Pickering and his mother, and Eliza's censure of his inhumane treatment of her as a 'thing' powerfully critiques academic and scientific moral disengagement. In the end,

Eliza forges an identity of her own, apart from the figure Higgins creates and beyond the reach of his authority:

> Oh when I think of myself crawling under your feet and being
> trampled on and called names, when all the time I had only to lift
> up my finger to be as good as you, I could just kick myself.

She refuses to return to her father or go back to Higgins's laboratory, and *Pygmalion* concludes with another doll slamming the door of her (now former) house.

Shaw underscored the importance of this empathetic capacity that Higgins lacks by disclosing the future choices of Clara Eynsford-Hill, who later is shocked to discover Eliza's humble origins. After plunging into the work of John Galsworthy and H. G. Wells and becoming aware of her own social privilege, she decides to reject

> the dungeon in which she had languished for so many unhappy
> years [which] had been unlocked all this time [and within which]
> the impulses she had so carefully struggled with and stifled for the
> sake of keeping well with society [turned out to be] precisely those
> by which alone she could have come into any sort of sincere human
> contact.

For Shaw, the breaking down of artificially created barriers between people has no value if it doesn't bring people closer to one another.

When *Pygmalion* reached the English stage in 1914, just as he had been concerned over the distracting comedy of *Arms and the Man*, Shaw was anxious that, as he wrote to his wife, the opening night audience 'laughed themselves into such utter abandonment and disorder that it was really doubtful for some time whether they could recover themselves and let the play go on'. In addition, controversy immediately erupted over Eliza's infamously blunt response to the prospect of walking home by herself through the park: 'Not bloody likely!' Indignant ire over the line from the city's politicians and clergy was vigorously stoked by the newspapers and certainly fuelled ticket sales and electrified playgoers. While Shaw as always thrilled to public scraps over his writing, he was disappointed in this case that it swirled around the more prurient than substantive aspects of his play. In any case, however, *Pygmalion* was and remains a critical and popular smash.

In his choice of 'A Romance' as a subtitle, Shaw used the word in the Shakespearian sense to emphasize the 'exceedingly improbable ... transfiguration' at the play's core, with a nod towards the Ovidian mythological roots of the play's title. He was determined to discourage any prospect of a romantic relationship between Higgins and Eliza, but audience expectations and a degree of improvisation on the part of the actors who originated the roles in London threatened to sentimentalize the ending. In response, Shaw's prose 'sequel'—first published with the script in 1916—finds Eliza definite and explicit in rejecting a 'lifetime of fetching Higgins' slippers [in favour of] a lifetime of Freddy fetching hers'. The postscript begins:

> The rest of the story need not be shewn in action, and indeed,
> would hardly need telling if our imaginations were not so enfeebled
> by their lazy dependence on the ready-mades and reach-me-downs
> of the ragshop in which Romance keeps its stock of 'happy endings'
> to mis fit all stories.... People in all directions have assumed, for no
> other reason than that she became the heroine of a romance, that
> she must have married the hero of it. This is unbearable [because]
> Eliza, in telling Higgins she would not marry him if he asked her,
> was not being coquettish: she was announcing a well-considered
> decision.

Furthermore, although she remains bound to Pickering, who initially finances her South Kensington florist shop, Shaw makes clear that the success of Eliza's enterprise eventually clears that debt.

Personally and professionally, Eliza determines her own future, but the middle-class respectability and marriage she chooses hardly challenge the gender and class systems, situating the character alongside Gloria Clandon and *Man and Superman*'s Ann Whitefield rather than Vivie Warren and Ibsen's Nora Helmer.

Despite the pointed addition to its literary version, the playscript remained unchanged, and Shaw could not dampen the enthusiasm of audiences and theatre companies that this Pygmalion would marry his Galatea. When the opportunity to revise the play for the cinema arrived in the 1930s, Shaw took another shot at honing the script to establish the authoritative ending he desired and ward off those pesky Cinderella strains; unbeknownst to him, though, a second ending to the film was shot that definitively brought Eliza back to Higgins and his slippers. The Academy Award he won in 1938 for the screenplay was poor compensation for the retro-fitting of Eliza from assertive and successful business owner to subservient wife. While Shaw always resisted efforts to turn *Pygmalion* into a musical, after his death, Alan Jay Lerner and Frederick Loewe adapted the screenplay—replete with its romantic ending—into their enormously successful *My Fair Lady*, whose initial productions in New York (1956) and London (1958) had record setting runs and whose film version won eight Academy Awards in 1964.

All of Shaw's 'pleasant' comedies are often revived and always cherished, and the playwright learned quickly how to work, Fabian-like, within the structures and expectations of middle-class comedy to articulate his views on bourgeois morality and the dangers of fossilized idealism. These plays brought him considerable financial success, especially in America, and widespread recognition as a leading dramatist. The beginning of the new century would be a turning point for the playwright as he sought to represent on the stage the step that follows disillusionment (the trope that threads his *Unpleasant* and

Pleasant volumes) on the path forward through social reform to true human advancement. In that endeavour, Shaw's distinctive brand of comedy will aid him in formulating a wider vision of what he called Creative Evolution, a process that operates under the aegis of the Life Force to countervail the challenges of human ignorance, obstinacy, and fallibility.

Chapter 4
'Puritan'

If, for all of his clowning as GBS, Shaw took his comedy seriously as a tool of reform, every theatrical genre was an opportunity to cultivate intellectual enquiry and critical scrutiny in audiences (Figure 5). In 1901, he published *The Devil's Disciple*, *Caesar and Cleopatra*, and *Captain Brassbound's Conversion* together in a volume he titled *Three Plays for Puritans*. They were written for, in his words,

> a generation [steeped in error] that is thoroughly moralized and
> patriotized, that conceives virtuous indignation as spiritually
> nutritious, that murders the murderer and robs the thief, that
> grovels before all sorts of ideals, social, military, ecclesiastical, royal
> and divine.

Yet in a sense Shaw too was a Puritan, habitually railing against the romanticizing or glorifying of middle-class moral ideals, advocating integrity over hypocrisy, and practising strict fidelity to a core set of animating principles. As G. K. Chesterton put it,

> Bernard Shaw exhibits all that is purest in the Puritan; the desire to
> see truth face to face even if it slay us, the high impatience with
> irrelevant sentiment or obstructive symbol; the constant effort to
> keep the soul at its highest pressure and speed. His instincts upon
> all social customs and questions are Puritan.

5. Portrait, *circa* 1904.

Puritans are further distinguished by their ardent adherence to a larger theological vision, and Shaw's religion, christened 'Creative Evolution' in 1916, was variously (and sometimes contradictorily) formulated throughout his life, its doctrine drawing upon strains from the writings of Charles Darwin, Jean-Baptiste Lamarck, Arthur Schopenhauer, and Friedrich Nietzsche. As biographer A. M. Gibbs writes, the main thrust of his ideas about religion…was that the godhead is not a perfect, complete, and unchanging entity but rather an evolving phenomenon. The universe is driven by an intelligent, purposive force, the Life Force, which strives towards higher forms of life and consciousness through the processes of evolution.…In this gospel according to Shaw, the purpose of human life is to *contribute* to the evolution of the godhead, of which we indeed are a part.

The energy of the Life Force animates species-wide intellectual, spiritual, and moral growth, spurred through the procreative laboratory of marriage and activated by the agency of extraordinary individuals, within whom works (as one character describes it) 'Life's incessant aspiration to higher organization, wider, deeper, intenser self-consciousness, and clearer self-understanding'. Shaw's ambition to create a 'big book of devotion for modern people' that chronicled the aegis of the Life Force was fortified by an evangelism that would yoke all of his varied writings.

Unfortunately, ignorance coupled with human propensities for revolt and failure perpetually thwart the project of Creative Evolution. As he described it in *Pen Portraits and Reviews* (1931), 'the creative Energy, as yet neither omnipotent nor omniscient, but ever striving to be both, proceeds by the method of trial and error'. As such, our task, as Shaw understood it, is to arrange our mindset and our institutions not only to stay out of the way of the Life Force but to cultivate living conditions so as to enable its progressive harvest. In the theatre, he believed, since 'there can be no new drama without a new philosophy', playwrights 'must rewrite all the old plays in terms of their own philosophy'. *Man and Superman*, described by its author as both a 'comedy' *and* a 'philosophy', ambitiously strives to map the workings of Shaw's cosmology and remains one of his absolute best plays.

Man and Superman (1901–2)

The play starts with John Tanner, a young Socialist armchair revolutionary, and conservative lawyer Roebuck Ramsden each bewildered to discover that they have been appointed joint guardians of Ann Whitefield by the terms of her late father's will. Shaw further complicates the situation when Ann's determination to wed Tanner becomes clear. A staunch critic of marriage and sentimental delusions, he flees from her to the Continent in his motor car, inverting conventional gender roles that prescribe the female as the pursued rather than the romantic pursuer. Later, camped among a group of anarchist brigands led by the colourful and charismatic Hector Mendoza, Tanner drifts into an overnight dream that imagines an extended debate among figures that blend *Man and Superman* characters with those from Mozart's *Don Giovanni*. Mendoza becomes the Devil, and Tanner becomes Don Juan; Dona Anna is Ann, and the Statue is a re-envisioning of Ramsden. In what Shaw termed a 'Shavio-Socratic dialogue [thrust] into [his] perfectly modern three-act play', Heaven and Hell are *chosen* destinations based on one's particular values and cast in typically Shavian opposition: realism, vision, and purpose (Heaven) and idealism, pleasure, and sentiment (Hell). The protracted and wide-ranging discussion runs the gamut of many familiar Shavian topics but works especially to clarify Shaw's religion. In an essay written a decade later titled 'The Religion of the Future', he explains:

> I believe the universe is being driven by a force that we might call the Life Force. We are all experiments in the direction of making God. What God is doing is making himself, trying to improve himself, from being just a mere powerless will or force. This force has implanted in our minds the ideal of God. We are not very successful attempts at God so far, but...there never will be a God unless we make one...we are the instruments through which that ideal is trying to make itself a reality.

In the dream, Don Juan emulates the figure of the 'philosophic man who seeks in contemplation to discover the inner will of the world, in invention, to discover the means of fulfilling that will, and in action to do that will by the so-discovered means'. Shaw promotes striving to ignore petty distractions and reject self-delusions and committing oneself to a higher calling that obligates one to improve social conditions so that progress of the godhead (inherent within all of us) can occur unimpeded. Too often, though, human beings are perversely committed in the opposite direction. As the Devil observes,

> the power that governs the earth is not the power of Life but of Death; and the inner need that has nerved Life to the effort of organizing itself into the human being is not the need for higher life but for a more efficient engine of destruction. The plague, the famine, the earthquake, the tempest were too spasmodic in their action; the tiger and crocodile were too easily satiated and not cruel enough: something more constantly, more ruthlessly, more ingeniously destructive was needed; and that something was Man, the inventor of the rack, the stake, the gallows, and the electrocutor; of the sword and gun; above all, of justice, duty, patriotism and all the other isms by which even those who are clever enough to be humanely disposed are persuaded to become the most destructive of all the destroyers.

To combat this cynicism, Don Juan carves out a strategy for spurring progress, feeding the mind to contravene the human bent towards self-sabotage:

> Man gives every reason for his conduct save one, every excuse for his crimes save one, every plea for his safety save one; and that one is his cowardice. Yet all his civilization is founded on his cowardice, on his abject tameness, which he calls his respectability. There are limits to what a mule or an ass will stand; but Man will suffer himself to be degraded until his vileness becomes so loathsome to his oppressors that they themselves are forced to reform it.... [But] the most surprising part of the whole business [is] that you can make any one of these cowards brave by simply putting an idea into his head.

The following morning, Ann arrives with a second group of travellers, and both cars continue on to Granada where Tanner can no longer evade Ann's matrimonial advances, ruefully declaring that 'the trap was laid from the beginning... by the Life Force':

> Marriage is to me apostasy, profanation of the sanctuary of my soul, violation of my manhood, sale of my birthright, shameful surrender, ignominious capitulation, acceptance of defeat. I shall decay like a thing that has served its purpose and is done with; I shall change from a man with a future to a man with a past; I shall see in the greasy eyes of all the other husbands their relief at the arrival of a new prisoner to share their ignominy.... The Life Force. I am in the grip of the Life Force...

Evoking the struggle of Gloria Clandon in *You Never Can Tell* whose rationality is unprepared for the explosion of feeling, he declares:

> I love you. The Life Force enchants me; I have the whole world in my arms when I clasp you. But I am fighting for my freedom, for my honor, for my self, one and indivisible.

In this case, it is the man who must reconcile the loss of his esteemed independence as the 'marked down victim, the destined prey'.

While she is unable to articulate it fully, Ann is fully in tune with the Life Force working through her to powerfully craft natural selection. At the end of the play, she swoons, overcome, her 'pulse positively bounding', with Tanner describing her as 'only triumphant, successful, victorious' but cautioning that it 'is not happiness, but the price for which the strong sell their happiness'. Despite being conquered, Tanner resolves, with Ann's blessing, to 'go on talking' and vows immediately to sell all the material goods they will receive as wedding gifts to fund the printing and free circulation of his 'Revolutionist's Handbook', a treatise which the playwright actually included in the 1903 published edition. As he outlines in its dedication, Shaw crafted the play as a 'dramatic parable of Creative Evolution' in which the conventional marital closure becomes an evolutionary foundry for social reform and advancement:

> [*Man and Superman* is] a stage projection of the tragi-comic love chase of the man by the woman; and my Don Juan is the quarry instead of the huntsman. . . . The woman's need of him to enable her to carry on Nature's most urgent work, does not prevail against him until his resistance gathers her energy to a climax at which she dares to throw away her customary exploitations of the conventional affectionate and dutiful poses, and claim him by natural right for a purpose that far transcends their mortal personal purposes.

In this formulation of marriage as Life Force workshop, the woman is 'breaking out of the Doll's House and asserting herself as an individual instead of a mere item in a moral pageant' while the man is 'selected by Nature to carry on the work of building up an intellectual consciousness of her own instinctive purpose'. With Ann and Tanner, Shaw further refines the prototype he created with Gloria and Valentine in *You Never Can Tell*, each bringing to the marriage distinct, desirable qualities that quite literally sow the seeds for a gradual attainment to a more profound level of consciousness.

Only a few years prior to *Man and Superman*, Shaw himself had finally entered the institution. Charlotte Payne-Townshend, a 38-year-old high-born Irish intellectual who liked to attend Fabian meetings in London, met Shaw in January 1896, after which their relationship deepened only in fits and starts because of the demands of his speaking, reviewing, and playwriting commitments as well as his residual involvement in other romantic entanglements. However, late that summer, they spent much of six weeks walking and talking together as guests of Fabian friends Sidney and Beatrice Webb at a cottage in Suffolk, and letters exchanged the following autumn indicate a sincere connection had formed. An inveterate and intelligent reader, writer, and activist, Charlotte shared much common ground with Shaw, and they remained close over the next year and a half, going to lectures, performances, and meetings. Even as it grew more serious, both were ambivalent about marriage, and Shaw bristled much like the characters in some of his comedies, against the perceived threat to individual agency that the arrangement posed to both of them, writing to Charlotte: 'No: you don't love me one little bit. All that is nature, instinct, sex: it proves nothing beyond itself. Don't fall in love: be your own, not mine or anyone else's.'

Sounding a bit like Gloria Clandon or Ann Whitefield, Charlotte resolved to break the stalemate by proposing to Shaw herself, a gesture which he rejected. When she travelled to Rome in March of 1898, he missed her immensely. His health problems, including exhaustion from his breakneck schedule and an infected foot which eventually required surgery, seemed to intensify their drawing together. With the groom on crutches (that two weeks later would cause a fall down the stairs and a broken arm), the wedding took place on 1 June 1898, with husband and wife both 41 years old. Charlotte immediately took charge of Shaw's physical recovery and ably managed his professional schedule. Near the beginning of *Man and Superman*, Tanner warns a friend keen on marriage about the danger at hand: 'Of all human struggles there is none so treacherous and remorseless as the struggle between the artist man and the mother woman.' Be that as it may, the Shaws would remain together for the next forty-five years.

The Royal Court Theatre (1904–7)

With *Man and Superman*, Shaw honed his distinctive blend of comedy; with its 'Don Juan in Hell' dream sequence, he perfected his technique of staging the discussion of ideas in place of plot progression, a dramaturgical trademark that would be most fully realized in his Edwardian plays *John Bull's Other Island*, *Major Barbara*, *Getting Married*, and *Misalliance*.

Dovetailing with his ongoing political activism during this time, Shaw reaffirmed the stage as a pre-eminent site for the consideration of pressing social issues and finally secured a proper venue to expose a wider section of the theatregoing public to his drama in performance. Across three seasons at the Royal Court Theatre, 70 per cent of the nearly 1,000 productions staged were of Shaw plays and became the genesis of what critic Max Beerbohm (who had taken over Shaw's *Saturday Review* position) termed the 'fashionable craze' for Shaw's plays.

In the early summer of 1900, Shaw met Harley Granville-Barker, a young, gifted actor who would go on to play iconic roles in Shaw's plays (many for the first time in public performance), including Frank Gardner in *Mrs Warren's Profession*, Marchbanks in *Candida*, Dubedat in *The Doctor's Dilemma*, Father Keegan in *John Bull's Other Island*, Tanner in *Man and Superman*, and Cusins in *Major Barbara*. The intelligent and industrious Granville-Barker agreed with Shaw about the corruption of Shakespeare on the popular stage and was instrumental in re-envisioning the ways in which the Bard's plays were approached by actors and seen by audiences. As Shaw had quickly discovered, contemporary plays that, in form and content, adhered to principles of what was called the New Drama were either non-starters or difficult sells for the commercial theatre, controlled by conservative audiences, egocentric actor-managers, stagecraft mired in melodramatic convention, and an emphasis on opulent set and costume design. Experimental ventures in the 1890s, including the Stage Society, which had produced five of Shaw's plays for licensing performances, were created by theatre practitioners who sought to produce more purposeful and socially relevant plays but could do so only in very limited ways to avoid government censure. Similar to what Shaw had championed frequently in his criticism, Granville-Barker had a vision of a permanent public theatre that would cultivate a regular audience for new plays from among those frustrated with the vapid but fashionable West End offerings. Programmed by Granville-Barker and his business manager John E. Vedrenne, the Royal Court Theatre in Sloane Square soon became a pilot venture, and its productions were lauded by reviewers and attracted diverse audiences, hungry for excellent acting and intellectual entertainment.

For the first time, Shaw had a directorial and administrative hand in the enterprise so that he could cast smart and versatile actors skilled in diction and open politically and artistically to the challenging ideas his work presented. (Many were fellow Fabians.) In addition to premieres and revivals of Shaw's plays, the Court was instrumental in providing an excellent outlet for other emerging playwrights committed to innovative styles and urgent social issues, including Elizabeth Robins's important suffrage play *Votes for Women!*, groundbreaking naturalistic drama from Barker himself, and new translations of Greek tragedies and contemporary European plays. Crafting ensemble-based, modestly designed stagings, the repertory favoured short performance runs that demanded of company members rigour and risk-taking. The first year of the Royal Court venture saw the premiere of *Man and Superman* as well as two more plays by Shaw that continue his enquiry into how the institutions of worldly power can best be of service to the Life Force. If *Man and Superman* charted its workings on a personal level within the context of marriage, *Major Barbara* and *John Bull's Other Island* ponder the ethical arrangement of political and spiritual authority in society to prepare the way for true evolutionary advancement.

John Bull's Other Island (1904)

At the turn of the 20th century, the literary side of the Celtic Renaissance encouraged native writers and artists to infuse

Gaelic language, contemporary politics, and elements of Irish folklore into their creative work. Shaw was ambivalent about the movement's nationalism and self-romanticizing, especially concerned that they could feed intra-society prejudice and political violence. But he finally got around to realizing his intention to write a play about Ireland in 1904, what he called his 'political farce' *John Bull's Other Island*. It was greatly admired by William Butler Yeats, who then was collaborating with Lady Gregory on what would eventually become the Abbey Theatre, but its casting and design challenges proved insurmountable for their novice company. *John Bull's* received its original production as Shaw's initial new contribution to Granville-Barker's tenure at the Royal Court and proved very successful through five separate stagings between 1904 and 1906. Prime Minister Arthur J. Balfour attended five performances, and King Edward VII famously is alleged to have laughed so hard one night that he broke his chair. It would be the actor who originated the role of Tom Broadbent who would eventually get the play performed in Dublin in 1907 (albeit by an English company) where it also enjoyed acclaim.

Infused with what Yeats called Shaw's 'geographical conscience', *John Bull's* is the study of a joint business venture undertaken by Broadbent and Larry Doyle, two civil engineers who seek to seize mortgaged farmland on which the owners have defaulted to develop the rural town of Roscullen into a tourist destination for foreign travellers. Broadbent is an Englishman whose perception of Ireland borrows from music hall stereotypes while Doyle is an expatriate Irishman who rejects romance in favour of realism, bitterly pushing back against his upbringing in Roscullen. At the centre of their colonial encounter is Peter Keegan, a priest defrocked for granting absolution to a Hindu and now a visionary wanderer who strives to harness spiritual and political power towards the advancement of peace and human progress. Keegan's utopian sensibility is at odds with Broadbent's materialist faith in the salvation of entrepreneurial investment, in this case a vacation resort draped in manufactured 'authentic' Irishness. With *John*

Bull's, Shaw is able to critique Anglo-Irish relations, especially the exploitation exerted by the bigger island upon the smaller that was legitimized by a framework of dehumanizing tropes of Irishness and John Bull stereotypes within English imperial discourse, sentimental fiction, and the 19th-century stage.

Major Barbara (1905)

Like Vivie Warren, Barbara Undershaft's journey of discovery in *Major Barbara* turns upon her disillusionment with regard to family money. Fittingly, Shaw's original title was *Andrew Undershaft's Profession,* but his decision to rename the play denotes another shift in dramaturgical focus away from that initial 'problem play' paradigm. For sure, the middle act of *Major Barbara,* set in a Salvation Army shelter, is the socialist realist still speaking, but Shaw's utopian thinking comes to the forefront of its final scene, expanding the scope beyond the mere exposure of immoral economics. *Major Barbara* explicitly weighs a progressive solution, seeking a way forward beyond Vivie's individual rejection of her mother and the atrophied systemic toxicity that concludes *Widowers' Houses.*

Subtitled 'a discussion in three acts' and occurring over a span of just three days, *Major Barbara* begins in the library of a fashionable London home and finds Lady Britomart Undershaft with a dilemma: both of her daughters are engaged to men who are unable to sufficiently support them. To secure a fiscal settlement for them, she has been forced to reach out to her estranged husband Andrew, who has made a fortune as an arms manufacturer. Barbara, the elder, disavows the trappings of her comfortable drawing room existence in favour of active social work, choosing to dismiss her maid, become a major in the Salvation Army, and pledge to live on a poverty-level wage with her fiancé, classics scholar Adolphus Cusins. The second act takes place at Barbara's public shelter, located in an area of London where a third of residents lived in extreme poverty and currently on the verge of being shuttered due to a lack of funding. The news that it has been saved by enormous donations from Sir Horace Bodger, a whisky distiller, and from Andrew himself prompts Barbara to resign in disgust at the prospect of operating on the profits of alcohol and the instruments of violence. She is shocked to discover that her beloved Army depends upon industrial monies to function, subsisting on the fruits of the capitalism that victimizes the very class to which it ministers.

At the end of the play, the family returns from their tour of the Undershaft munitions factory, quite surprised by the high standards of working and living Andrew has created for his employees. The conversation then shifts to the settlement of the Undershaft inheritance on Cusins, which includes the business as well as the engineered company town Perivale St. Andrews, a 'spotlessly clean' community replete with affordable food and housing and rich in intellectual, leisure, and even spiritual amenities. Andrew's industrial vision, characterized by Cusins as 'horribly, frightfully, immorally, unanswerably perfect', revises the usual, ruthlessly exploitative 'sweatshop' mentality into one that prioritizes the workers' long-term productivity by providing them with the means to lead stable, fulfilling lives, starting with a living wage. As Shaw writes in the preface, 'security, the chief pretense of civilization, cannot exist where the worst of dangers, the danger of poverty, hangs over everyone's head'; for him, intellectual and spiritual advancement of the species can only be achieved when material resources are certain and sustained for all. As Undershaft says to his daughter,

> food, clothing, firing, rent, taxes, respectability, and children. Nothing can lift those seven millstones from man's neck, but money; and the spirit cannot soar until the millstones are lifted.

Typical of Shaw's technique, Andrew, the war profiteer and ostensible villain, is, as the playwright describes him, 'intellectually and spiritually as well as practically conscious of the irresistible natural truth which we all abhor and repudiate: to wit, that the greatest of our evils, and the worse of our crimes is poverty'. The character devilishly demonstrates to his daughter and prospective son-in-law how his munitions factory contributes more substantively to the well-being of his workers than Barbara's army. For Shaw, the Christian charity organization founded in 1881 by William Booth to combat poverty and minister to the urban poor was well intentioned but misdirected, leveraging symptoms to gain converts rather than addressing the root of a systemic problem. He didn't believe that the poor were a necessary if pitiful by-product of society so a focus on saving souls neglected a responsibility to their suffering bodies. The substitution of an idealized 'great family of mankind under the fatherhood of God' belied, for Shaw, the evils of an earthly hierarchy that could be conscientiously reformed.

With renewed vigour, Barbara ultimately is energized by the evangelical opportunities the environment of Perivale St. Andrews provides, where conversion can happen without having to resort to taking advantage of the desperation of the destitute. She disdainfully indicts what she and Cusins might have been in the Army—'very superior persons, and neither of us a bit of use'. Their inheritance enables them, as Undershaft says, 'to turn [their] oughts into shalls'. Both realize that power is needed to combat the abuses of authority; as Undershaft points out to Cusins at the shelter, 'honour, justice, truth, love, mercy' can only be afforded on the backs of 'money and gunpowder'. 'Money controls morality,' Shaw wrote in his second novel *The Irrational Knot* (1880), and 'all sound and successful personal and national morality should have this fact for its basis'. In accepting the munitions business, Cusins says that he is selling his soul for 'neither money nor position nor comfort, but for reality and for power…a power simple enough for common men to use, yet strong enough to force the intellectual oligarchy to use its genius for the general good'. In that sense, Barbara and Cusins represent a step forward from Undershaft's profit-driven practicality, bringing to the enterprise an activist ethic, what Cusins calls 'making war on war'. The couple agrees that 'the way of life [is] through the factory of death', 'through the raising of hell to heaven and of man to God, through the unveiling of an eternal light in the Valley of the Shadow'.

If the earlier plays that confronted poverty such as *Widowers' Houses* and *Mrs Warren's Profession* aimed for a general awakening of the audience to Fabian activism, *Major Barbara* contemplates a Marxist tempering of capitalism itself as a particular solution. In a section of the preface entitled 'The Gospel of St. Andrew Undershaft', Shaw writes:

> The universal regard for money is the one hopeful fact in our civilization, the one sound spot in our civilization....Money is the most important thing in the world. It represents health, strength, honor, generosity, and beauty as conspicuously and undeniably as the want of it represents illness, weakness, disgrace, meanness, and ugliness....And the evil to be attacked is not sin, suffering, greed, priestcraft, demagogy, monopoly, ignorance, drink, war, pestilence, nor any other of the scapegoats which reformers sacrifice, but simply poverty.

Too often, Shaw felt, reform movements got caught up in ministering to the effects and thus diverted from a singular quest to eliminate the cause. Of course, the pursuit of money on its own can become mercenary and amoral without being harnessed with a conscience, precisely what Cusins and Barbara bring to the enterprise as inheritors of Perivale St. Andrews. *Man and Superman's* John Tanner and Ann Whitefield are thus recast outside the drawing room and outside the conventions of comedy, situated within a real world context and endowed with a more expansive social vision, conjoining the political ethos of Shaw's early drama with his experiments in 'comedies of ideas'. In a 1909 letter to author Henry James, he wrote:

I, as a Socialist, have had to preach, as much as anyone, the enormous power of the environment. We can change it; we must change it; there is absolutely no other sense in life than the task of changing it. What is the use of writing plays, what is the use of writing anything, if there is not a will which finally moulds chaos itself into a race of gods.

The Edwardian era was a golden age for Shaw, replete with groundbreaking new plays and productions of old ones coupled with an ever-expanding level of international celebrity that made him a sought-after commentator on every major issue, trend, and phenomenon of the time. Politically speaking, the period also saw some legislative gains—expanded protection for civil disobedience and ratification of unemployment insurance, minimum wage, workers' compensation, and pension laws. While the kind of social change Shaw advocated was being implemented, the pace was slow and even stalled on reforms he felt were shamefully overdue such as women's equality and Home Rule for Ireland. The impending war would corrode further his already weakened faith in gradualist Fabian tactics and indeed in even the abilities of the Life Force to overcome human misguidedness, stubbornness, and self-destructiveness. Despite Shaw's dexterity at marshalling controversy towards meaningful dialogue and cultural advancement, a crisis just on the horizon would threaten the very presence of GBS in the public realm and test his abilities to persevere in his ardent evangelism.

Chapter 5
'Political'

For Shaw, politics and religion were intimately intertwined in that the world had to be arranged in ways that aided the Life Force in its work; thus, a secular game plan was necessary to complement his cosmology. While he chooses the word 'political' as a subtitle for just four of them, every one of his plays is not only stoutly engaged with specific issues of his time but wholly invested in exploring the question of how to organize ourselves most equitably and most productively. Even before the outbreak of world war, the Victorian answer to that question seemed perilously close to unravelling. In the first decade of the new century, almost a quarter of the planet and its inhabitants were subject to Britain's imperial control. Nonetheless, serious fault lines were undeniably appearing, including labour strife (ripe with the possibility of a major multi-industrial strike), increasingly militant demonstrations by women's suffrage activists at home and by independence groups in Egypt and India, and a prospective civil war in Ireland. In retrospect, though, the Edwardian and Georgian periods would be considered the twilight of the old order, their relative stability brilliantly infused with flashes of modernity in politics, ideas, and technology. Shaw's plays during this time mark the full development of his unique, hybrid 'dramaturgy of ideas' always in dynamic, prickly engagement with the most current events and controversies.

The advent of the Great War dramatically exploded traditional ways of mapping the world and humanity's place in it, lasting four long years and inaugurating new styles of battle with trench warfare and advanced weaponry including machine guns, tanks, bombs, and nerve gas. At the same time, Modernist innovation in painting, music, and literature prioritized the fracturing of conventional form in an effort to 'make it new' and speak more resonantly to a new normal, to which 19th-century intellectual, moral, and artistic traditions seemed at best irrelevant and at worst tyrannical. The catastrophe would similarly divert Shaw's playwriting in new directions even as it maintained its investment in exposing the ways in which the caste system, idealism, and capitalism conspire to derail the process of Creative Evolution. Before those theatrical masterworks arrive, though, it is Shaw's journalism that takes centre stage to castigate British nationalism and foreign policy, boldly assigning culpability for the conflict to failed government leadership on both sides.

Common Sense about the War (1914)

When fighting broke out, Shaw, who had already been a stalwart critic of foreign policy in the press, immediately began writing what would become an eighty-four-page essay that purported to 'talk and write soberly about the war'; *Common Sense about the War* was published in the 14 November 1914 issue of the *New Statesman*. In the pamphlet, he provides an 'alternative' genealogy of the war, advice on how to fight it, and a plan for how to prevent such a debacle from happening again in the future. 'Nations are like bees,' Shaw wrote: 'they cannot kill except at the cost of their own lives.' He blamed the horrific conflict on the militarist and nationalist interests present in the governments of *both* Britain and Germany and public support for it on a deliberate campaign of propaganda waged throughout the popular media:

Neither England nor Germany must claim any moral superiority [since] both were engaged for years in a race for armaments [and] both still indulge in literary and oratorical provocation.

He indicts the military-industrial complex, responsible for the stockpiling of armaments and expansion of the armed forces, warning readers against buying into the spin that the war came about because of England's heroic response to German aggression in Belgium.

While he argues that, since it has been started, the conflict needs to be fought vigorously, Shaw considers it imperative in the step following victory to 'democratize our diplomacy if we desire peace'. For him, hope was contingent upon purging economic and industrial profiteering interests from foreign policy negotiations and removing blundering aristocrats from positions of government and military authority. In negotiating an armistice, he wrote,

we must remember that if this war does not make an end of war in the west, our allies of today may be our enemies of tomorrow as they are of yesterday, and our enemies of today our allies of tomorrow as they are of yesterday; so that if we aim merely at a fresh balance of military power, we are likely as not to negotiate our own destruction.

Most directly, Shaw vehemently charged: 'We began it; and if they met us half-way, as they certainly did, it is not for us to reproach them.'

Because he viewed the war as one in which the working class were commanded to the front lines to arbitrate a dispute among the elites, part of reconstruction for Shaw was the establishment of a Socialist democracy to replace a divided social structure within which the seeds of such discord are sown. He appealed to those members of

George Bernard Shaw

the solid, skeptical, sensible residuum who know the value of their lives and services and liberties, and will not give them except on substantial and honourable conditions. These Ironsides know that it is one thing to fight for your country, and quite another to let your wife and children starve to save our rich idlers from a rise in the supertax.

He further condemned the ways in which the event was packaged and sold as a 'beneficent gymnastic, moral or spiritual', to a frightened and uncritical public (especially in recruitment and fundraising campaigns) by the government and popular press; 'war as a school of character and nurse of virtue, must be formally shut up and discharged by all the belligerents when this war is over'. The summer of 1914 became the urgent occasion for which GBS had been preparing in his nearly three decades of public advocacy, and the stakes had never been higher as he leveraged the authority of his media presence and the credibility of his brand. As scholar Nelson O'Ceallaigh Ritschel writes, '*Common Sense* remains today, in fact is ageless, as a model of the questioning and criticizing that is not only needed in a free press, but is the only and ultimate guarantee of a democratic society.' Unfortunately, as much as Shaw's responsible citizenship and many of his analytical insights were spot on, his timing was way off.

The blame Shaw assigned in *Common Sense* to the popular press all but ensured that the essay's reception would be hostile, and the playwright became the *ad hominem* target of attacks from all sides (Figure 6). The flurry of subsequent published pieces (including responses from Shaw to those who denounced him) made international news, and the playwright found himself swept up in a controversy that threatened everything he had achieved. On both sides of the Atlantic, his reputation as a public advocate was suddenly at odds with being branded a traitor in many circles. Theatres opted not to produce his plays, and libraries and bookstores in Britain and North America

6. 'George Bernard Shaw' (1928) by Dorothy Wilding.

removed his work from their shelves. Personally, he found himself thrown out of organizations and losing longstanding close relationships, his commentary perceived as the ravings of, as H. G. Wells put it, 'an idiot child laughing in a hospital'. Undaunted, Shaw continued to write copiously on the war, attempting to clarify and further develop earlier positions concerning strategic success and the brokering of a non-recriminative peace to include the reform of the social conditions and institutions that were for him the true causes. As the casualty count skyrocketed and the horrors of the bloodshed became more evident, Shaw's views would later be reconsidered by journalists and activists. In 1931, he published *What I Really Wrote about the War*, and the *Saturday Review* commented that it was 'as applauded [now] as it was condemned and despised during the war years'.

Considering the explosive blowback from *Common Sense*, it is surprising both that the British army turned to Shaw in the summer of 1915 to boost flagging enlistment totals in Ireland and that they were surprised that what they got back was not an inspirational affirmation of the war effort. With his one-act play 'O'Flaherty V.C.', Shaw rejected the patriotic jingoism of recruiting drives and proposed an alternative marketing strategy to 'appeal to [the Irishman's] discontent, his deadly boredom, his thwarted curiosity and desire for change and adventure'. In other words, as he wrote in the preface, Irish recruitment will be successful when it seeks to capitalize on the fact that 'an Irishman's hopes and ambitions turn on his opportunities of getting out of Ireland'. The play's central figure is a battlefield hero named Dennis O'Flaherty, whose experiences at the front have spawned very anti-romantic views of war and make him at best a reluctant celebrity leading home front parades and delivering platform speeches at recruitment drives. Indeed, across much of his writing at the time, Shaw relentlessly sought to awaken a public gulled by sentimental propaganda. Unfortunately, strongly influenced by the military authorities who were concerned that the play might spark violence or be exploited by the enemy, the planned premiere of 'O'Flaherty V.C.' at the Abbey Theatre was cancelled.

As the war persisted and much of what he had written about its causes and effects proved to be prophetic, Shaw still found his brand tarnished, the prophet-sharing potential of his powerful media platform diminished, and his optimism seriously challenged in the face of such an abominable calamity. While his journalism illustrated his immediate and direct response to the war, his major plays throughout the 1920s also are composed in its long shadow and vitalized by many of the same principles that had garnered such an incendiary response.

Heartbreak House (1916–17)

In *Heartbreak House*, Shaw sought to customize a portion of his *Common Sense* argument for the stage, in particular his critique of a singular social sphere, what he called 'cultured leisured Europe', that he felt had let go the reins during the run-up to war. Heavily influenced by a staging of Anton Chekhov's *The Cherry Orchard* he saw in London, Shaw's 'fantasia in the Russian manner' depicts the vapid interactions of a tragically self-involved ruling class residing in an Edwardian country house that resembles 'an old-fashioned high-pooped ship with a stern gallery' and literalizes a foundered ship of state. Expounding at length upon the causes and corrosive effects of war, not only on life but on the arts, its preface envisions two 'houses' existing in a state of utter futility that together embody the lethal disconnect between 'power and culture'. Heartbreak House is filled with the

> only repositories of culture who had social opportunities of contact with our politicians, administrators, and newspaper proprietors, or any chance of sharing or influencing their activities. But they shrank from that contact. They hated politics. They did not wish to realize Utopia for the common people: they wished to realize their favorite fictions and poems in their own lives; and, when they could, they lived without scruple on incomes which they did nothing to earn.... They took the only part of our society in which there was leisure for high culture, and made it an economic, political, and, as far as practicable, a moral vacuum.

Its counterpart Horseback Hall is 'a prison for horses with an annex for the ladies and gentlemen who rode them, hunted them, talked about them, bought them and sold them, and gave nine-tenths of their lives to them, dividing the other tenth between charity, churchgoing (as a substitute for religion), and conservative electioneering (as a substitute for politics)'. Between the 'two atmospheres', Shaw charges, 'it is hard to say which was the more fatal to statesmanship'. *Heartbreak House* would not appear publicly until after the war, eventually published in 1919 but not produced until 1920. Since then, it is frequently revived and considered by many to be Shaw's magnum opus for the stage.

Blending elements of manners comedy and farce with extensive discussion, *Heartbreak House* begins with the awakening of Ellie Dunn, a young girl who has fallen asleep at the door of a country house while waiting to be received. The mistress of the house, Hesione Hushabye, has invited her for the weekend, along with her father Mazzini and her older fiancé Boss Mangan, a wealthy entrepreneur who ruined Dunn's business. Ellie is stunned by the house's unconventionality, the lack of attention to proper etiquette and hosting of guests, and the lukewarm reception for Ariadne, Hesione's sister who has been abroad for twenty-three years with her husband, 'the Governor of all the Crown colonies in succession'. As the play progresses, Hesione successfully breaks the engagement as Mangan swiftly succumbs to her charms; for her part, Ellie has fallen in love with Hesione's husband Hector, whom she has unknowingly met before. Presiding over the goings on is Hesione's father, an 88-year-old retired sea captain and inventor who sharply disapproves of the other characters' 'foolish lives of romance and sentiment and snobbery'. Ominously, this 'soul's prison' of a residence subsists on income derived by the sale of patents for Captain Shotover's experimental designs for explosives, lifeboats, weapons to combat tanks and submarines, and even a 'mind-ray'. Like Andrew Undershaft, Shotover is a war profiteer, infusing the play retroactively with the spectre of the twelve million human casualties of the Great War. The presence of Mangan and Ariadne connects the privilege of the household to predatory capitalism and imperial subjugation as *Heartbreak House* incriminates the system of values of a spiritually and morally bankrupt culture refusing to see its complicity in the infirmities of the world as it drifts towards disaster.

Besides a cascade of guest arrivals, the play's slight plot contains a scene of hypnosis, an attempted burglary, much Chekhovian frustrated desire, and of course lots of talk about many of the usual Shavian topics including love, money, dreams, beauty, and marriage. Throughout, there is an unusual somnambulant quality to the characters who, as one points out, 'have been too long in the house' and thus 'haunt it' rather than live in it. The audience's experience of the play is equally surreal. Critic Ronald Bryden suggests that the play 'unmoors' itself to arrive at its ultimate dramatic destination:

> What begins as an Edwardian comedy lifted out of its period, to float in a timeless twentieth-century mixture of disillusion and presentiments of disaster, ends in the present with bombs raining down on England.

The onstage air raid in act three, when a zeppelin begins dropping bombs around the characters, who have gathered in the garden outside the house, was inspired by the playwright's experience of two German warships passing above his house in Ayot St Lawrence.

When the assault begins, Mangan and the burglar ('the two practical men of business') flee and perish in an explosion that also destroys the local rector. Perversely, the rest of the alienated and bored characters welcome the attack, eagerly turning on the house's lights in order to make themselves a clearer target and deeming the sound of the explosions a 'splendid drumming in the sky...like an orchestra[,] like Beethoven'.

The disillusionment of heartbreak, which Shaw sees as the first step in a larger process that moves towards altruistic social reform, is a familiar experience for many of his characters, including Harry Trench, Vivie Warren, and Barbara Undershaft, as well as a primary objective in both his dramaturgy and his political writings for his audiences and readers. Ellie discloses late in the second act that, following her heartbreak, she feels 'stripped of everything, even of hope', as if there 'is nothing [she] could not do, because [she wants] nothing'. While Shotover praises her sensibility as 'genius' and 'the only real strength', Ellie remains captive to spiritual atrophy.

Following her disappointment at the disconnect between the actual Hector and her romanticization of him, she ponders marrying Mangan not for love but for a security that will allow her to escape reality into a world of art and leisure. But Shotover warns her:

> If you sell yourself, you deal your soul a blow that all the books and pictures and concerts and scenery in the world won't heal....You are going to let the fear of poverty govern your life; and your reward will be that you will eat, but you will not live.

In the last act, Ellie reveals that she has consecrated her relationship with Shotover, that she has given her 'broken heart' and 'strong sound soul to its natural captain, its spiritual husband and second father'. For Shaw, the painful shedding of self-delusions and the subsequent refusal to idealize flawed and immoral institutions, practices, and ideas are essential to prepare the way forward.

As Hesione and Ellie hope for another air raid the following evening, though, indicative of the depths of disaffection and self-destruction to which the culture has sunk, the surviving residents of Heartbreak House remain resolute in their holding pattern, as if the Creative Evolution Shaw has for so long worked to further has come to a dead end, as if the 'drumming in the sky' is

> Heaven's threatening growl of disgust at us futile creatures [that indicates] either out of that darkness some new creature will come to supplant us as we have supplanted the animals, or the heavens will fall in thunder and destroy us.

The seeming inability of human beings in positions of cultural authority to manage government and leadership humanely and salubriously along with the stubborn consistency with which they commit acts of atrocity against one another led Shaw into despair that, left to their own devices, ordinary people could and would never evolve. *Heartbreak House*'s hallucinogenic style and its deep cynicism are precisely what make the play, as scholar Eric Bentley termed it, 'the nightmare of a Fabian'. What were needed, in Shaw's view, were pro-active individuals of extraordinary quality to marshal the resigned multitudes towards higher states of wisdom and endeavour. As Captain Shotover entreats: 'Navigation. Learn it and live; or leave it and be damned.'

Back to Methuselah (1918–20)

Back to Methuselah is Shaw's most ambitious play in scope. In it, he sought to dramatize on a much larger temporal and spatial scale the working of the Life Force, beyond what he had done with *Man and Superman*. In the play's preface, written a decade later, he recalled that

> the exuberance of 1901 [had] aged into the garrulity of 1930; and the war has been a stern intimation that the matter is not one to be trifled with. I abandon the legend of Don Juan with its erotic associations, and go back to the legend of the Garden of Eden [with] this my beginning of a Bible for Creative Evolution.

He was striving to 'fulfill [his] natural function as an artist' and be 'an iconographer of the religion of [his] time' with a cycle of five plays, termed a 'Meta-Biological Pentateuch' and starting with Adam, Eve, and the serpent in 4004 BC. The second play jumps forward to the present and centres around a proposal made by two brothers (a philosopher and a biologist) to two politicians that the human lifespan must be extended to 300 years, if the problems raised by the war in addition to those endemic to the human character are to be adequately resolved. Two minor characters from that play, the maid and the curate, re-emerge as political leaders in the third, set in Britain in the 22nd century, when the first of the desired 'long-livers' appear, even as the self-governance of the culture has got worse. The fourth play takes place in the year 3000 around Galway as the long-livers have finally superseded the short-livers. Shaw considers its plot a 'tragedy' as an elderly gentleman eventually dies of 'discouragement' when he realizes that he is unable to adhere to the values of the long-livers. That pessimism is given full expression by one of the long-livers who refers back to an age characterized by the development of weapons of mass destruction, including gas, automatic guns, and eventually atomic bombs:

> A thousand years ago, when the whole world was given over to you shortlived people, there was a war called the War to end War. In the war that followed it, the capital cities of the world were wiped out of existence; and that was the end of pseudo-Christian civilization.... You will wipe yourselves out just as you did before. You will then begin all over again as half-starved ignorant savages, and fight with boomerangs and poisoned arrows until you work up to high explosives once more, with the same result.

As he wrote in *Common Sense*, the species has undermined itself 'by inventing weapons capable of destroying civilization faster than we can produce men who can be trusted to use them wisely'.

The challenge faced by Creative Evolution is to break this entropic spiral, *and Back to Methuselah*'s final play, titled 'As Far As Thought Can Reach', takes place in AD 31920, when, 'after passing a million goals', human beings 'press on to the goal of redemption from the flesh, to the vortex freed from matter, to the whirlpool in pure intelligence'. At this stage, humans hatch from eggs as teenagers and quickly mature into solely cerebral entities that exist for centuries, free of the constraint of bodies and emotions. The Life Force continues to exert its influence as an innate impulse that urges the species, as scholar John Barnes puts it, 'to replace a universe that was all matter with one that will be all mind'. Sceptically utopian at best in its long view, its most advanced humans exuding traits both laudable and imperious, *Back to Methuselah* proceeds from the playwright's deep despondency and floundering belief in the efficacy of participatory democracy. The only will that can triumph is the Life Force, and human beings, if they are to endure and evolve at all, must be saved from themselves. The play's prodigious canvas is essential as Shaw demonstrates how 'we are made wise not by the recollections of our past but by the responsibilities of our future'.

Saint Joan (1923)

When he recasts the 15th-century journey of Joan of Arc, Shaw walks a similar tightrope between abject pessimism and desperate hope for those who seem innately equipped to lead humanity in the right direction. He called *Saint Joan* a 'chronicle play' but mindfully sidesteps not only what he felt were misrepresentations of Joan's story in many accounts but also the stage conventions of historical melodrama. Dismissing sentimental romance and martial spectacle, Shaw centres six episodic scenes followed by an epilogue around an individual nourished, as biographer A. M. Gibbs puts it, by a 'social and religious vision in which the common people have spiritual sovereignty over the dominions and powers of the political and ecclesiastical hierarchies of worldly institutions'.

Joan had been envisioned in the popular imagination as *both* a New Woman and a traditional feminine exemplar and was claimed as a fitting advertisement for a variety of causes, including French nationalists, the American military, and temperance and suffrage groups. For Shaw, it was her encounter with the most powerful institutional forces of her time that was most interesting, as he felt her story really *began* with her execution and concluded with her canonization by the Catholic Church in 1920. In the play's preface, he describes Joan as a 'sane and shrewd country girl of extraordinary strength of mind and hardihood of body':

> Everything she did was thoroughly calculated; and though the process was so rapid that she was hardly conscious of it, and ascribed it all to her voices, she was a woman of policy and not of blind impulse.

She is for Shaw a true vessel of the Life Force—determined, charismatic, and courageous. His characterization renders her at once a mystic visionary like Peter Keegan and a practical revolutionary threatening the authority of Church and state, one who is often not aware of how radical a challenge she poses. Her determination to restore the integrity of France and her populism are directly at odds with the stakeholders in English imperialism and Catholic dogma. Joan's struggle is that which attends all activists and their movements but, more particularly, embodies the clash of nationalism and aggression that had led to the slaughter of the Great War. In Shaw's eyes, Joan's story could not have been more relevant or needed in 'a world situation in which we see whole peoples perishing and dragging us toward the abyss which has swallowed them, all for want of any grasp of the political forces that move civilization'.

In a programme note for the original English production, Shaw justified his departures from the historical record as well as from contemporary popular accounts and asserted that the presence of the epilogue is what elevates the play from being 'only a sensational tale of a girl who was burnt, leaving the spectators plunged in horror, despairing of humanity'. Rather, 'the true tale of Saint Joan is a tale with a glorious ending; and any play that did not make this clear would be an insult to her memory'. The dialogue in the first six scenes further seeks to emphasize connections between Joan's time and the 20th century through, as one critic of the first English production noted, 'the extraordinary mixture of archaic language, modern English and current slang'. In the epilogue, Shaw experiments as he had in 'Don Juan in Hell' with the conceit of a dream to extend Joan's presence and influence vividly into the post-war era. He underscores the departure in style of the play's conclusion through the innovative use of other stage languages, including sound, lighting, and projections.

The epilogue initially takes place a quarter of a century after Joan's execution as the main characters visit the former Dauphin and culminates in the arrival of a messenger dressed in modern garb who announces the canonization. Later, left alone on the stage alongside the sleeping King Charles, Joan exclaims: 'O God that made this beautiful earth, when will it ever be ready to receive thy Saints? How long, O Lord, how long?' Echoing Job, it is a provocative question and one that was at the forefront of the playwright's mind, disappointed as he was at the doggedness of social iniquity and suffering as well as the ongoing failure of democratic governments to address them effectively. The opportunity that post-war rebuilding offered was being squandered by what Shaw termed 'the eternal war between those who are in the world for what they can get out of it and those who are in the world to make it a better place for everybody to live in'.

Global celebrity and a Nobel Prize

After cool and often bewildered receptions for *Heartbreak House* and *Back to Methuselah*, *Saint Joan* was an immediate international sensation and solidified its author as Britain's pre-eminent playwright and GBS its premier public intellectual. His celebrity was rapidly becoming global due to exposure not simply through mass periodicals but via the airwaves and celluloid. Although a performed speech from *Man and Superman* was part of a radio bill that occurred in 1923 without Shaw's permission, a broadcast reading of 'O'Flaherty V.C.' in November 1924 that featured the playwright voicing all the parts would officially launch his relationship with the BBC, through which he exponentially widened his audience. Over the course of the next twenty-five years, those who were not theatregoers for temperamental, financial, or geographic reasons could experience Shaw's language through public radio and later television broadcasts of his plays (starting with a two-evening *Saint Joan* in the spring of 1929) and even occasional GBS cameos giving a speech or participating in a debate. An avid moviegoer, Shaw also gleefully revelled in a Movietone News short filmed in 1928 at his house in Ayot St Lawrence. He would go on to be directly involved in translating half a dozen of his plays to the screen, including *Major Barbara* (1941), *Caesar and Cleopatra* (1945), and most notably *Pygmalion* (1938), for which he won his Oscar for Best Screenplay. He also would travel extensively during the next few years, and his visits to countries such as China, India, the United States, Japan, Russia, South Africa, and New Zealand were frequently elaborate affairs that put him in close contact with powerful leaders and were always covered extensively by the local and international press and often captured by newsreel cameras.

If GBS's reputation was shaky after *Common Sense*, by all accounts, Shaw had become a national institution by the end of the 1920s and one of the most famous public figures in the world. The same year that *Mrs Warren's Profession* was finally afforded its first public performance in England, Shaw was awarded the Nobel Prize in Literature for 1925, accepting it only because Charlotte reminded him what it would do for the reputation of Ireland. He donated the prize money to establish a foundation to translate the work of Swedish writers into English (beginning with plays by August Strindberg). While he turned down offers of a knighthood and the Order of Merit, Shaw never flagged in putting his gigantic platform to good use on behalf of social and political reform. In 1928, he wrote *The Intelligent Woman's Guide to Capitalism and Socialism*, to provide, as had Karl Marx, shrewd analysis of the shortcomings of capitalism and proposals of more equitable alternatives. The *Guide* eventually became the very first title published by Pelican Books, an offshoot of Penguin, intended to provide the public with a series of accessible volumes on non-fictional topics. In it, Shaw crafted the case for his Socialist principles to appeal to the general reader and avoided the dull theoretical jargon of academic textbooks in favour of his clever trademark style. As a result, the *Guide* sold tremendously well, the initial print run selling out immediately and spawning subsequent editions in both Britain and the United States. While he would later expand it and produce a denser companion volume titled *Everybody's Political What's What* (1944), the original *Guide* remained, in treatment and substance, the best distillation of a majority of his core principles.

Too True to Be Good (1931)

Too True to Be Good, the final of Shaw's Great War plays, features two veterans as leading characters and experiments in form infused by the disorientation and apprehension that characterized the 1920s. It is indeed the best of the 'extravagant' late plays characterized, according to A. M. Gibbs, by 'exotic settings and fantastical incidents and characters, with frequent complete departures from the conventions of naturalism'. *Too True to Be Good* begins in familiar enough territory, a well-appointed suburban bedroom containing a patient 'with an unhealthy complexion', but immediately takes a surreal turn when a Microbe enters that 'in shape and size resembles a human being; but in substance ... seems to be made of a luminous jelly with a visible skeleton of short black rods'. Speaking directly to the audience and echoing the playwright's decades-long critique of the medical industry, the outraged germ inveighs against the doctors who have fallaciously blamed it for the wealthy young woman's illness:

> Measles: that's what she's got. . . . And she's given them to me, a poor innocent microbe that never did her any harm. And she says I gave them to her. Oh, is this justice? . . . These humans are full of horrid

diseases: they infect us poor microbes with them; and you doctors pretend that it is we that infect them.

It becomes apparent that the true source of her infirmity is the toxic lifestyle of her socio-economic class. As she sleeps, former combat airman turned burglar Aubrey Bagot attempts to steal the Patient's pearl and diamond necklace. An ersatz clergyman, Bagot is soon able to renew through vigorous preaching the Patient's vitality by inciting her to rebel against what she calls her 'slavery' to the class and gender system. Together with his partner in crime and ex-nurse Sweetie, he convinces the girl to stage her own kidnapping so that all three can escape and support themselves with the proceeds of robbery and blackmail. Following the Patient's 'emancipation from this wretched home', the Microbe suddenly reappears, itself also mysteriously cured, and puckishly declares 'the play [to be] now virtually over [even though] the characters will discuss it at great length for two acts more', pointedly advising the audience that 'the exit doors are in order'. If the curtain line is good for a jab at the playwright's expense, it also sets up the audience's expectations for what will follow. While there is of course quite a lot of conversation in store, the play's setting takes a couple of radical turns. The first occurs when the two remaining acts abruptly shift their scene to a 'military cantonment [on a] sea beach in a mountainous country'. At the very edges of the Empire, the characters don various disguises as traditional hierarchies and stable identifies collapse, and they find themselves 'falling endlessly and hopelessly through a void in which they can find no footing'.

The second shift happens in the play's final moments when, without answers and without direction, Bagot delivers a 'torrent of sermons' directly to the audience as he and the already sparse scenic elements gradually become enveloped by an 'impenetrable fog':

I am ignorant: I have lost my nerve and am intimidated: all I know is that I must find the way of life, for myself and all of us, or we shall surely perish. And meanwhile my gift has possession of me: I must preach and preach and preach no matter how late the hour and how short the day, no matter whether I have nothing to say—

A stunning contrast to John Tanner's ongoing talking at the end of *Man and Superman*, this conclusion is a powerful expression of the frightening bewilderment of the time and the desperate need for something to believe in following the disintegration of, as scholar Peter Gahan terms them, the old 'grand narratives' of the time, including Shaw's own 'religion of Creative Evolution [and] political doctrine of socialism'. Gone is the Life Force's confident sanctifying of the way forward, and in its place is what one character refers to as a 'bottomless abyss' of empty talk. With the former ways of organizing existence in ruins (not to mention the typical conventions of the theatre) and Bagot's voice fading from the stage, the audience is left shaken and perplexed in the fog. The world represented in *Too True to Be Good* is one in which, as one character succinctly observes, 'the institutions are rocking and splitting and sundering' and there is no place 'to live, no certainties, no workable morality, no heaven, no hell, no commandments, and no God'. In short, 'the universe is wrecked', and Shaw's daring departures in dramaturgical style sought to mirror the unsettled confusion of the 1920s. A critic for *The Times* complained of the play's 'formless' structure, lacking 'beginning, middle, and end', that rendered it 'an undigested notebook… a few notes in a wilderness of fantastic irrelevance'.

Although Bagot's words soon become unintelligible to the theatregoers, Shaw provides access in the published edition of the play to the full text of the character's concluding speech, at least to the way it 'would probably run' and what the response will be:

> *The audience disperses (or the reader puts down the book) impressed in the English manner with the Pentecostal flame and the echo from the Lord's Prayer.*

On the page, Shaw proceeds to undercut the preacher and his preaching, stating that 'fine words butter no parsnips [because] any rascal who happens also to be a windbag can get a prodigious volume of talk out of [the Pentecostal flame] without ever going near enough to be shriveled up'. The script's final paragraph ends the play by directing the reader to a character other than Bagot, asserting that

> the author, though himself a professional talk maker, does not believe that the world can be saved by talk alone. He has given the rascal the last word; but his own favorite is the woman of action.

The end of the Patient's journey through the play is less dramatic than Bagot's, as her mother at last catches up with her and negotiates a new relationship for them that is fulfilling and equitable. Having grown weary of Bagot's preaching and 'being devoured by parasites', the Patient, craving 'something sensible to do', forges an 'unladylike sisterhood' with her mother 'to clean up this filthy world and keep it clean'. Regarding Bagot, hearkening back to Ann Whitefield's confidence, she possesses a 'cheerful conviction that the lost dogs always find their own way home ... *if* the women go out and look for them'. Despite so much adversity and desolation, what Bagot simply describes as 'the way of life' and what Shaw will call in *On the Rocks* the 'evolutionary appetite' still endures. While Shaw's favoured 'woman of action' will roar to power again in his next play *The Millionairess*, this optimistic reassertion of the Life Force at work (at least among the women) is notably absent from *Too True to Be Good* in performance, as its bleak and terrifying stage conclusion encapsulates the unravelling of traditional beliefs, values, and theatrical forms between the wars but at the same time creates a space that a new generation of avant-garde writers and theorists of the drama will take as their starting point, led by Antonin Artaud and Samuel Beckett.

In a short essay entitled 'Peace Conference Hints' (1919), Shaw warned that narrativizing any war as one would a melodrama was most dangerous when the guns are silenced and treaties were negotiating the new world order. Villainizing and punishing the losers would foment 'another Armageddon, with poison gas, infected microbes, and all sorts of horrors'. Needless to say, Shaw was prophetic. The antagonistic power struggle that had engendered the conflict continued into its adjudication of peace. The process was hijacked as an opportunity for retribution, with the Allies demanding reparations from an economically incapacitated Germany rather than working collaboratively to rebuild Europe for the benefit of all of its residents. In just a few years, Britain would once again find itself engaged in another war with an embittered, imperialist Germany martialled by a new brand of authoritarian leadership that would wholly seize Shaw's attention.

Chapter 6
'Extravagant'

As Shaw's notions about evolving British drama didn't stop with simply changing *what* plays should do but extended to *how* they should they do it, generalizing about the form of Shaw's more than fifty plays is a nearly impossible task since truly no two are alike. Fittingly, he used the word 'extravagant' to describe the flexibility in structure and style of three of his late plays—*The Apple Cart* (1928), *Too True to be Good* (1931), and *Geneva* (1936). However, Shaw's penchant for experimentation in these areas was evident from the start of his career, even before the theatre. His early novels possess what scholar Richard Farr Dietrich calls a 'hybrid and unique form, a crazy-quilt' of traditional and avant-garde narrative elements that anticipate seminal Modernist work by James Joyce and Gertrude Stein.

When he turned to writing for the stage, he worked, like William Shakespeare, within multiple genres, including comedy, tragedy, and the history play, but also worked *across* them, spinning ideas in a dialectic dance with one another that didn't just challenge conventional boundaries of form but actively reconfigured them. Eschewing the formula of what was called the 'cup-and-saucer' realism of 19th-century plays and casting aside their sentimentality and default affirmations of middle-class morality, he turned tropes from melodrama and farce inside out so that, rather than drive the action, they provided merely the occasion for the exchange of perspectives anchored by the 'real world' experience of characters. While he believed strongly that the connection between what happened on the stage and what was happening outside the theatre needed to be vibrant and strong, merely 'holding up the mirror to Nature' was inadequate. In a 1908 speech titled 'Literature and Art', Shaw shared his understanding of the craft:

> [The Playwright] is to take the events of life out of the accidental, irrelevant, chaotic way in which they happen, and to rearrange them in such a way as to reveal their essential and spiritual relations to one another. Leaving out all that is irrelevant, he has to connect the significant facts by chains of reasoning, and also to make, as it were, bridges of feeling between them by a sort of ladder, get the whole thing in a connected form into your head, and give you a spiritual, political, social, or religious consciousness.

His refusal to follow prescribed modes or prevailing trends, his determination to ignore expectations dictated by propriety, and his perseverance in creatively roaming out of bounds together make his dramaturgy flagrantly extravagant and the ideal forum for the intellectual whirlwind of his dialogue.

Following the Great War, Shaw was also stepping beyond the confines of his Fabian Socialism, which had long represented for him the most ethical means of social design, braced within a democracy by impassioned debate among competing visions for change.

In an 1891 tract, Shaw wrote that 'the Fabian Society, having learned from experience that Socialists cannot have their own way in everything any more than other people, recognizes that in a Democratic community compromise is a necessary condition of political progress'. Yet, it hardly seems the same author who, decades later, fashions three of his late plays as direct meditations on governmental leadership that considers totalitarianism.

The Apple Cart, On the Rocks (1933), and *Geneva* were written at a time when Shaw seriously pondered the efficacy of enlightened authoritarian government with regard to accelerating advancement of the species and placed desperate faith in the particular brand of 'Superman' that arose on the continent between the wars.

World betterers

Fuelled by his post-war cynicism, his impatience with the way in which democracy was being practised and with the sluggish Fabian process of social change, he continued to express optimism about the Soviet experiment because it seemed to realize his Shavian theory about the relationship between Creative Evolution and so-called 'world betterers'. For decades, Shaw had disagreed with prominent Fabians like Sidney Webb who believed that the individual was always secondary to the will of the collective. *Everybody's Political What's What* (1944) contains amplified calls for reform of the British governmental system threaded with admiring remarks about Joseph Stalin. Needless to say, Shaw's politics were complicated, but his utopian thinking remained a staple throughout, even if his preferred engine for cultural renovation changed.

Since the turn of the 20th century, Shaw had been anxious over how effective the Fabian method of reform could be if the democracy itself was dysfunctional. John Tanner's 'Revolutionist's Handbook', included by Shaw in the published edition of *Man and Superman*, posits that 'democracy substitutes election by the incompetent many for appointment by the corrupt few'. The futility of Heartbreak Houses and the tragedy of Joan are indications of the scepticism and despair Shaw felt following the Great War, especially as the prospect of a second global conflict became all but a certainty. In the 1920s and 1930s, Shaw grew increasingly restless over an inefficient legislative process, undermined by corrupt or incompetent officials and a chronically, even wilfully uninformed electorate. How could the West learn from their mistakes, especially while the version of democracy being practised remained so far short of the Fabian vision of responsible government and so unable to effectively manage economic challenges such as steadily rising unemployment, stagnant industrial growth, and worldwide economic depression? As the Devil opines in 'Don Juan in Hell', humankind is 'the most destructive of the destroyers', incapable of meaningful progress and, left on its own, risks becoming an evolutionary dead-end. In a piece for the *Humane Review*, Shaw wrote in 1901 that, if 'English civilization is at the end of its tether...the tether can only be lengthened by the substitution for those artless grown-up children of a quite different sort of Englishman'—one who can return the wheels to progressive motion on the right track.

Informed by Marx's concept of force as a means of social betterment, Shaw's so-called 'world betterer' was an evolutionary figure endowed with greater clarity of purpose and strength of commitment to 'the unflinching recognition of the facts' than everyone else. His Superman refuses the distraction of vapid middle-class idealism and trite emotionalism, the safety of how things are, and seeks to realize a larger vision, precisely in tune with the Life Force; as Shaw wrote in *The Quintessence*, 'he who can see that not on Olympus, not nailed to the cross, but in himself is God: he is the man to build [the] bridge between the flesh and the spirit, establishing his third empire in which spirit shall not be unknown, nor the flesh starved, nor the will tortured and baffled'. If the concept of the Superman was borrowed from Nietzsche's *Thus Spoke Zarathustra*, Shaw revises through a number of various writings his predecessor's isolated, austere hero into a charismatic leader in direct and robust engagement with the surrounding world. Unsurprisingly, this special individual crops up in Shaw's plays quite frequently and serves as an index for Shaw's unfolding views on the means of evolutionary advancement, including his voiced support of rising authoritarian leaders in Europe who initially seemed to provide post-war stability and a roadmap to national recovery.

If comedy provided a canvas for Shaw to trace the stealthy operations of the Life Force through conspicuous sexual selection as in *Man and Superman*, another genre proved useful in first bringing the superman character to stage life. *Arms and the Man* is technically Shaw's first history play, set in 1885 and written probably in response to the November 1893 death of Alexander of Battenberg. Critic Ronald Bryden argues that Shaw's counterbalancing of Bluntschli and Sergius in that play is 'at once a comedy of a perfect rationalist—Shaw's first sketch of a Superman—who points where the world must go, and the tragedy of a heroic romantic who embodies what the world will lose by going there'. It is the former figure that would become a revered character in the Shavian imagination, a world betterer who charismatically moves systemic critique from the realm of talk to that of forceful action, actively aiding the Life Force in spurring Creative Evolution. 'The best governors', Shaw maintained, 'will not accept any control except that of their own consciences.'

Men of destiny

Just as an affinity for penning popular history plays helped establish Shakespeare's reputation in the late 16th century, Shaw turned to the genre in the 1890s to gain recognition as an important new voice in late Victorian theatre, although at first glance his efforts seem in their form very consistent with the melodramatic stage spectacles Shaw the critic routinely denounced. Long before telling Joan's story, Shaw was fascinated by commanding historical figures and includes in *The Devil's Disciple* (1896) a cameo appearance by General John Burgoyne, British commander of the ill-fated 1777 Saratoga campaign during the American Revolution. One of only two plays Shaw sets in America, *The Devil's Disciple* follows the exploits of Richard Dudgeon, a family ne'er do well who supports the rebellious colonists and criticizes the hypocrisy of puritanism. Witty, charming, and outspoken, Burgoyne is a formidable foil for Dudgeon, and Shaw includes him so that, in addition to triumphing over Victorian ideals of religion, morality, and love, the young reprobate would also prove 'superior to gentility—that is, to the whole ideal of modern society'. Yet, the scene-stealing general also castigates military and governmental bureaucracy and presciently anticipates what he calls the 'jobbery and snobbery, incompetence and Red Tape' that will eventually cost Britain its American colonies and the real Burgoyne his reputation.

The figure continues to evolve in *Caesar and Cleopatra* (1898), Shaw's first major play of ideas, in which he fashions a Julius Caesar that rebuked Shakespeare's 'conventional tyrant of the Elizabethan stage', bringing to stage life a man

> heroic in the true human fashion: that is touching the summits only at rare moments, and finding the proper level of all occasions, condescending with humour and good sense to the prosaic ones, as well as rising to the noble ones.

The play criticizes the shortcomings of the British Empire while venerating Caesar's expansive organizational and aspirational vision, which guides his mentorship of the teenage Cleopatra. When she fails the first test of altruistic and edified leadership, Caesar's lament seemingly forecasts the gloomy mood of *Heartbreak House*:

> And so to the end of history, murder shall breed murder, always in the name of right and honor and peace, until the gods are tired of blood and create a race that can understand.

Napoleon Bonaparte appears in *two* different plays by Shaw, the first a one-act written in 1895 titled 'The Man of Destiny' and subtitled a 'Fictitious Paragraph of History'. Set in Italy in 1796,

the young and as yet undistinguished Frenchman spars with a
clever young woman who has tricked a junior officer into turning
over his dispatches. While she is forced to give the letters back, she
stages a clever cross-dressing trick that outwits Napoleon as she
also holds her own throughout a fair amount of conversation with
him over a variety of topics, including his assertions about the
'stupid' English who are 'chained hand and foot by their morality
and respectability'.

If 'The Man of Destiny' reads as a trial run of sorts for the
exchanges between Ann and Tanner in *Man and Superman*, the
re-envisioning of Napoleon almost three decades later in *Back
to Methuselah* is indicative of Shaw's shift in focus away from
marriage as the crucible for Creative Evolution and towards
the directive navigation of the Superman. In contrast to the
earlier play, where the conqueror appears in nascent form, the
mature Napoleon 'marches with measured steps' into the
fourth part of *Back to Methuselah* and 'places his hand in his
lapel in the traditional manner', announcing, 'I am the Man of
Destiny':

> My talent possesses me. It is genius. It drives me to exercise it.
> I must exercise it. I am great when I exercise it.

The Oracle to which he presents himself is unimpressed however
and eventually horrified by his pompous warmongering. The
exercise of his genius means 'the shedding of oceans of blood, the
death of millions of men', and even Napoleon does not relish the
violence inherent to his talent 'to organize this slaughter':

> What satisfaction is it to me to see one fool pierce the entrails of
> another with a bayonet?...I must rule, because I am so superior to
> other men that it is intolerable to me to be misruled by them....
> I have the only imagination worth having: the power of imagining
> things as they are, even when I cannot see them....The value of
> human life is the value of the greatest living man....If you kill me,

or put a stop to my activity (it is the same thing), the nobler part of human life perishes.

As a composite figure of charismatic warrior-egotists (including Cain, who appears in the first part of *Back to Methuselah*), Napoleon is rebuked and humiliated by the Oracle. 'Much we care for his anger!' another character observes, 'War God indeed!'

While disgusted by the violence, Shaw, as scholar Matthew Yde writes,

> greatly admired the bold and assertive men of action who had embarked on political careers with the presumed intention of remaking the world for the better; these were provisional supermen [who would] clear the ground for the true supermen who evolve biologically in the distant future.

Manifestations of the superman figure had appeared in the Shavian utopian imagination as far back as *The Quintessence of Ibsenism* and *The Perfect Wagnerite*, preceding the varied stage incarnations of their counterparts that include the dominating arms manufacturer and social engineer Andrew Undershaft, who is lauded by his creator in the preface to *Major Barbara*, for 'his constant sense that he is only the instrument of a Will or a Life Force that uses him for purposes wider than his own'. Interestingly enough, though, it is a genealogy of *female* characters who act as theatrical stand-ins for the kind of authority figure whose presence expands in Shaw's political thinking after the Great War and challenge the gendered dictates of the superman concept.

Born bosses

Shaw's *Misalliance* (1909) epitomizes the full blossoming of Shaw's discussion idiom for drama, subtitled 'A Debate in One Sitting', and, like *Getting Married*, lacks any act/scene divisions. Up to his old tricks of mashing up melodramatic plot conventions,

Shaw crafts a distinctive blend of discourse, dysfunctionality, and disruption that swirls around various possible *mis*alliances between wan English characters visiting an Edwardian estate for the weekend. Shaw had initially entitled the play 'Just Exactly Nothing', and so unusual was its form that its original production was thwarted when the cast walked out in absolute confusion. For *The Times* theatre critic, *Misalliance* portrayed 'the debating society of a lunatic asylum—without a motion and without a chairman' and 'madness after all'. Shaw used the opportunity of the nearly 100-page preface to expound upon the relationship between parents and their offspring, denouncing the constraining obligation the ideology of the family exerts on children in addition to the oppressive institutionalization of learning and the horrors of punitive discipline. Besides its innovative form and style, which anticipate the mid-century advent of the Theatre of the Absurd, *Misalliance* marks a pivot in Shaw's evolutionary thinking.

The play takes place in the Surrey country house owned by John Tarleton, self-made underwear merchant whose success proceeds largely from shrewd mass-marketing practices. His daughter Hypatia, drifting into a passionless marriage, is bored by the endless and empty talk that fills the house, desperate for a break from the dull bourgeois routine:

> I'm fed up with nice things: with respectability, with propriety! When a woman has nothing to do, money and respectability mean that nothing is ever allowed to happen to her. I don't want to be good; and I don't want to be bad. I just don't want to be bothered about either good or bad. I want to be an active verb....I want to be; I want to do; and I'm game to suffer if it costs that....Home! Parents! Family! Duty! How I loathe them! How I'd like to see them all blown to bits!...I mean to make a fight for living.

Her father is unexpectedly prophetic when he says that his daughter is 'not satisfied. Restless. Wants things to Happen. Wants adventures to drop out of the sky.' Hypatia's revolutionary spirit is soon activated when an aeroplane crash-lands in the garden, shattering the greenhouse windows. Inside is Joey Percival, a virile young aviator, who immediately sparks her aggressive romantic pursuit, echoing Ann Whitefield's of Tanner. When determining arrangements for the coupling near the end of the play, the challenge of Percival's modest means is met by Hypatia's command to her father to 'buy the brute for me', a micro-repackaging of *Major Barbara* in its harnessing of capital to create optimum conditions for Creative Evolution. As Shaw writes in the play's preface, the proper way to view a child is as a 'fresh attempt to produce the just man made perfect: that is to make humanity divine'.

The deus ex machina that delivers a suitable mate to Hypatia also contains a second passenger, initially of indeterminate sex and unpronounceable name, to whom Shaw would later refer as 'the St. Joan of *Misalliance*'. A striking contrast to the effete English inhabitants of the Tarleton house, Polish acrobat Lina Szczepanowska is committed to risk-taking, self-conditioning, and individual autonomy, putting into daily practice her physical, spiritual, and mental agility:

George Bernard Shaw

> I am an honest woman: I earn my living. I am a free woman. I live
> in my own house. I am a woman of the world....I am strong: I am
> skilful: I am brave: I am independent: I am unbought: I am all
> that a woman ought to be.

Lina's powerful vitality both intimidates and attracts, as she dispatches the sexual advances from multiple male characters while searching for one truly willing to rise to the sublime challenge presented by the Life Force. Frustrated, at the end of the play, Lina expresses her desire to 'get out of this [stuffy house] into the air: right up into the blue' and selects Bentley Summerhays, Hypatia's anaemic and infantilized former suitor, to accompany her. Just as surprising as her choice is Bentley's willingness, despite his intense fear and anxiety, to take the risk and adopt her lifestyle and sensibility. After their departure, in contrast to the conclusion of *Man and Superman* where Tanner is encouraged to keep on talking, Tarleton declares that 'there is nothing more to be said', to which Hypatia replies, 'Thank goodness!'

Lina is a full incarnation of the Shavian world betterer—individuals incited by the Life Force into mesmerizing action that effectively transforms the administration of government and compels the governed to evolutionary growth. In the preface to *Saint Joan*, Shaw considers Joan in the same terms:

> She talked to and dealt with people of all classes, from laborers to kings, without embarrassment or affectation, and got them to do what she wanted when they were not afraid or corrupt. She could coax and she could hustle, her tongue having a soft side and a sharp edge. She was very capable: a born boss.

Shaw understands bossiness as a rare trait, one that must be tuned towards public service and collective progress rather than personal gain, and it is through this lens that he placed his fervent hopes in Stalin, Adolf Hitler, and Benito Mussolini to become the antidote to what he referred to as 'the mass of ignorance, weakness, and timidity' that was stalling genuine advancement. Soon, however, he would strongly criticize the latter two's virulent anti-Semitism as it became apparent in the early 1930s, an obsession he felt made both unfit to lead.

The title character of *The Millionairess* (1935), Epifania Ognisanti di Parerga Fitzfassenden, represents his fullest theatrical treatment of this 'boss'. Clearly an Undershaft descendant, this physically imposing and aggressive heiress possesses an astonishing proficiency at what scholar Margery Morgan calls 'organiz[ing] the productive capacities of others to multiply her wealth'. On her own, she is reckless, cruel, and unfocused. Her romantic counterpart, the Egyptian Doctor, is meant to remedy the capriciousness and aimlessness of the unchecked boss through altruistic ethical direction so that, in Shaw's words, 'decisions shall be made in the general interest and not solely in the immediate personal interest of the decider'. Like Jack Tanner, the Doctor initially resists the engagement but in the end is no match for Epifania's 'irresistible pulse'. The marriage that concludes *The Millionairess* mobilizes the impersonal and irresponsible brutality of capital in the service of the highest spiritual levels yet attained by human beings. Shaw, as he did in *Major Barbara*, proposes a strategic union that fuses wisdom and morality with resourcefulness and stamina to produce, in short, capitalism with a conscience. The newly wed couple resolves to recreate Britain into a 'Soviet Republic', wiping out 'poverty, dirt, disease, misery, and slavery' and creating wealth that will not be 'thrown away on idlers and their parasites' but benevolently distributed.

Late plays

Throughout the inter-war years, the world betterer and the governing style for which it comes to stand are prominent for Shaw, as his late discussion-centred plays that explicitly contemplate proper leadership are cast in the shadow of a parliamentary democracy struggling against myriad internal and external challenges. 'The riddle of how to choose a ruler is still unanswered,' he writes in *In Good King Charles's Golden Days* (1939), 'and it is the riddle of civilization.' The Russian experiment in communism drew Shaw's notice as, in theory, a much more equitable and practicable alternative for governance and social organization, one that he believed could prepare the way for Creative Evolution more efficiently, justly, and briskly. Set in the future, his play *The Apple Cart* uses a constitutional crisis (a king charged by ministers with exceeding his granted powers) as the context for an extended conversation about politics and especially the efficacy of a democracy run by a wealthy elite. The play flirts with the idea that a proper version of autocratic rule is a desirable by-product of the inevitable collapse of mismanaged, inefficient democracy. *On the Rocks* (Figure 7), which Shaw designated a

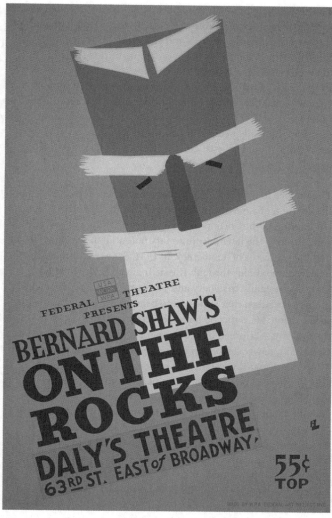

7. WPA poster for the 1938 Federal Theatre Project presentation of Shaw's *On the Rocks* at Daly's Theatre in New York City.

'political comedy', portrays a hapless Prime Minister called Sir Arthur Chavender as unable to cope with the pressing urgency of the current economic distress and ends with his resignation. At the same time, outside his office, a demonstration staged by the unemployed descends into a riot that must be violently put down by the police. An adviser urges the Prime Minister to support 'any Napoleon or Mussolini or Lenin or Chavender that has the stuff in him to take both the people and the spoilers and oppressors by the scruffs of their silly necks and just sling them into the way in which they should go with as many kicks as may be needful to make a thorough job of it'.

The preface to *On the Rocks* is infamous for its central tenet that the creation of a new, more robustly stable Britain necessitates the elimination of the uncooperative—shocking from a playwright so committed to the latent evolutionary potential in reasoned debate and the processes of democracy. In 1931, Shaw was treated to a heavily curated tour through Russia that carefully sanitized Stalin's systematic treachery and performed for the playwright a utopian socialism that appeared to beautifully realize his own social vision. He returned home to a country that seemed exactly the opposite—crippled by the financial and human costs of the Great War, newly steeped in the regressive economy of the Great Depression, and ravaged by mass unemployment, civic unrest, and widespread poverty. To many, parliamentary democracy, as it was being practised, seemed not strong enough nor astute enough to address these dire challenges, and, for Shaw, the crisis of leadership and an inevitable second world war called more urgently for a superman, whose strength of will could push forward and actualize a more effective government that would ensure equal opportunity and shared resources among its citizens. As its title *On the Rocks* suggests, Shaw felt the British ship of state had run aground, but, if its preface is a vehement, unilateral appeal, the play itself remains more consistent with Shaw's dramaturgical principles, allowing space for the exchange of alternative views, moments of optimism, and even some uncertainty about how to achieve the desired reform. 'Beware the pursuit of the Superman,' he wrote in 1902: 'it leads to an indiscriminate contempt for the human.'

A similar caution about the authoritarian project occurs in Shaw's most exotic play, *The Simpleton of the Unexpected Isles* (1934), which begins with a sad prologue set in a late 19th-century 'Emigration Office at a tropical port in the British Empire' and portrays the suicide of the young clerk. Eschewing realism for fable, the remaining acts depict a future experiment in eugenics conducted in an island garden and culminate in a visitation by an Angel to herald an apocalyptic Day of Judgement that will purge idlers and wastrels from the earth. The promise afforded by the utopian idealism that underwrites the island community at first seems fulfilled, but the play ultimately critiques imperialist assumptions and, even more interestingly, Fascist governmental presumptions, as the engineered offspring amorally and mindlessly submit to absolutist authority, chanting 'obedience is freedom from the intolerable fatigue of thought'.

Apocalypse also figures near the end of *Geneva*, set both at the League of Nations and at the World Court in The Hague. A decade or so before the Great War, Shaw conceived the idea of an international organization charged with maintaining global peace and invested with considerable authority. He worked together with fellow Fabians to sketch the contours of a body that could temper nationalism and competition to foster a climate of humanitarian cooperation and collaborative cultural, scientific, and artistic enterprise. *Geneva* turns upon a courtroom scene in which three dictators (thinly veiled versions of Hitler, Mussolini, and Francisco Franco by way of Commedia clowns) are brought to account for their actions. Yet, even as information about its humanitarian atrocities and horrific deprivations steadily emerged, Shaw continued to extol the virtues of Soviet government, and Stalin was spared direct inclusion in *Geneva*, although a Bolshevik 'Commissar' represents an unnamed fourth dictator.

After much discussion, the court proceedings are cut short when it is reported (later revealed, falsely) that the earth's orbit is 'jumping to its next quantum' and that all currently living things will be destroyed. In the decade following the play's premiere in 1938, Shaw would revise the script for each new production not only to reflect the progress of his own thinking on these figures but also to remain resonant with a world once again plunged into martial conflict. While initially optimistic, Shaw was disheartened when the enormous possibility of a League of Nations was undermined by the kind of administrative infirmities and wrongheaded thinking of which he was so critical in British government. 'They undertake to make a new world after every war,' he wrote, 'with hardly brains enough to manage a fried fish stall.'

This entwining of the political and the cosmological occasions Shaw's repeated turn towards the genre of the fable in his later work. Of course, he had great success with his 'Fable Play' *Androcles and the Lion* (1912), which, together with its extended preface, provides a context for Shaw to discuss theology and identify unifying principles and practices across belief systems to argue that 'there is only one religion, though there are a hundred versions of it'. Besides integrating elements of fable into *Back to Methuselah* and *Simpleton*, his 1932 short prose piece *The Adventures of the Black Girl in Her Search for God* depicts the eponymous hero on a quest that brings her into critical conversations with allegorical personifications drawn from religious mythology and philosophy, including an Irishman with grand ideas about Creative Evolution whom she eventually marries. *Farfetched Fables* (1948), one of his final works, is a linked series of short plays that attempt to further distil Shavian philosophy, repackaging and refining *Back to Methuselah* to an extent but setting the first fable just after the end of the Second World War. From there, the play depicts the formation of a disciplined world, scoured of intractable elements and poised for orderly and expeditious progress overseen by invisible advanced beings. To what degree Shaw's representations of these subjects were meant sincerely and to what degree satirically, in the vein of Jonathan Swift's *A Modest Proposal*, remains in contention among scholars and critics.

The world betterer makes a final appearance in Shaw's last full-length play *Buoyant Billions* (1946), which begins with a debate over whether Fabianism or Marxism provides the best model for progressive social change. Unexpectedly, the two characters in the play earmarked as ostensible supermen veer away from the realm of statecraft in favour of the field of research. The first gets waylaid in the middle of a global expedition to investigate atomic energy by another version of Ann Whitefield, to whom he is engaged by the final curtain. The youngest Buoyant child also initially declares himself a world betterer but is inspired by his brother's passionate speech about mathematics to switch his profession at the end of the play to that of scientist, embarking upon a search for the hormone that will evolve the species into a race of solely intellectual creatures. For Shaw, near the end of his life, it seems, as another character remarks, 'the future is with the learners' who alone can unlock the mysteries of the way forward. This final change of venue for world-bettering though is not as abrupt as it seems; in an October 1930 speech honouring Albert Einstein, Shaw pitched the same idea:

> Take the typical great man of our historical epoch and suppose that I had to rise here tonight and propose a toast to Napoleon. Well, undoubtedly, I could say many flattering things about Napoleon. But the one thing which I should not be able to say about him would perhaps be the most important thing. And that was that it would perhaps have been better for the human race if he had never been born. Napoleon, and other great men of his type, they were makers of empire. But there's an order of men who get beyond that.

They are not makers of empire, but they are makers of universe. And when they have made those universes, their hands are unstained by the blood of any human being on earth. Ptolemy made a universe that lasted 1400 years. Newton also made a universe which has lasted 300 years. Einstein has made a universe, and I can't tell you how long that will last.

Chapter 7
'Farfetched'

Pleasant and unpleasant, puritanical and political, GBS not only witnessed enormous cultural, political, artistic, industrial, and technological change throughout his ninety-four years but actively helped to shape how the key questions of the period were understood and deliberated. For the title of the 1948 allegorical digest of his beliefs *Farfetched Fables*, Shaw selected the adjective 'farfetched' not to suggest dubiousness or improbability but to describe the breadth of its mythic vision. The word is equally apt when applied to Shaw's own longevity, the scale of his thinking, and the extended, sustained reach of his prolific writing, arriving in the late 19th century, roaring through the 20th, and continuing to provoke into the 21st.

Facing increasing health challenges during the last years of his life, Shaw fell on 10 September 1950 while gardening and broke his thigh bone. Following surgery to repair it, he developed kidney and bladder issues that he was ultimately unable to overcome, passing away on 2 November. Three weeks later, his ashes were co-mingled with Charlotte's (who had died in 1943) and, at their house at Ayot St Lawrence, scattered, as biographer Sally Peters describes it,

> around the paths, the rose beds, the lawn-covered bank that held a
> bronze statue of Saint Joan, the earthly space in which the playwright
> had tilled the fertile garden of his imagination for half his long life.

Royalties from Shaw's plays had made him a very wealthy man; his estate, valued in 1950 at over £367,000, was among the largest in British literary history. His will made generous provisions for the Royal Academy of Dramatic Art, the British Museum where he had spent so much of his time studying, and the National Gallery of Ireland. Henry Higgins-like, Shaw also dedicated funds to the establishment of a new phonetic British alphabet that he hoped would create a mode of communication purged of dialect and hence the social class markers that he believed walled people apart from one another. Fortunately, he lived long enough to see the beginnings of the so-called 'welfare state' in England as, between 1945 and 1951, the Labour government actualized many core tenets of Shaw's social vision by bringing major industries (including coal, iron, steel, and transport), utilities, and the Bank of England under public ownership and creating a National Health Service, subsidized housing, and a national insurance system.

Recognition of Shaw as not only an enormously influential historical figure but also an important playwright began quite early, with biographies and critical monographs already appearing in the first two decades of the 20th century, even as he flippantly mused that

> my prophecies are forgotten in the excitement created by their fulfillment. That is the tragedy of my career.

Alongside other attempts in his final years to encapsulate the Shavian sensibility such as *Farfetched Fables* and *Everybody's Political What's What*, *Sixteen Self Sketches* (1949) indicates his investment in shaping how he would be remembered. While these autobiographical pieces (some new, some revised) have undeniably influenced the contours of our narrative of Shaw's life, they have had their reliability seriously questioned by biographers.

Arguably, though, Shaw had an eye on the long run very early on in his career, and his thoughts about the nature of a purposeful life *and* artistic afterlife often crop up in his commentaries about William Shakespeare. In the preface to *Man and Superman*, for instance, Shaw notes that

> Shakespear, with all his flashes and divinations, never understood virtue and courage, never conceived how any man who was not a fool could...look back from the brink of the river of death over the strife and labor of his pilgrimage, and say 'yet do I not repent me'; or, with the panache of a millionaire, bequeath 'my sword to him that shall succeed me in my pilgrimage, and my courage and skill to him that can get it.' This is the true joy in life, the being used for a purpose recognized by yourself as a mighty one; the being thoroughly worn out before you are thrown on the scrap heap; the being a force of Nature instead of a feverish selfish little clod of ailments and grievances complaining that the world will not devote itself to making you happy. And also the only real tragedy in life is the being used by personally minded men for purposes which you recognize to be base. All the rest is at worst mere misfortune or mortality: this alone is misery, slavery, hell on earth; and the revolt against it is the only force that offers a man's work to the poor artist, whom our personally minded rich people would so willingly employ as pander, buffoon, beauty monger, sentimentalizer, and the like.

While Shaw rarely passed up an opportunity to set himself above Shakespeare, when he expresses his own credo in 'The Sanity of Art' ('Any man who writes about himself and his own time is the only man who writes about all people and about all time'), it is certainly hard not to hear deliberate echoes of Ben Jonson's epitaph that deems the Bard 'not of an age, but for all time'. Indeed, Shaw's relationship with his vaunted predecessor, whom he condemned for a 'deficiency in that highest sphere of thought, in which poetry embraces religion, philosophy, morality, and the bearing of these on communities, which is sociology', is curiously ambivalent. His notorious skirmishes with Shakespeare's plays and posthumous reputation span Shaw's entire career and are,

8. Edwardian-era *Punch* cartoon by E. T. Reed entitled 'Design For A Statue Of "John Bull's Other Playwright" After Certain Hints By "G.B.S."'

on another level, a sustained meditation on the vexed legacy of a canonized playwright (Figure 8).

Bardolatry

Shaw couldn't deny the brilliant power of Shakespeare's language but was disappointed his plays did not follow the new style of drama that he championed, in forgoing the discussion of contemporary social problems for a focus on 'characters [who] have no religion, no politics, no conscience, no hope, no convictions of any sort'. Often proclaiming Ibsen's superiority on these grounds, Shaw faults Shakespeare for lacking a desire for reform behind his gift for verse and for what he called his 'barren pessimism', especially evident in the tragedies and romances, which depict such profound flaws in human nature. In the *Saturday Review*, he complained that to encounter 'utterances' such as

> 'Out, out brief candle,' and 'The rest is silence,' and 'We are such stuff as dreams are made of; and our little life is rounded by a sleep' is to turn from life, strength, resolution, morning air and eternal youth, to the terrors of a drunken nightmare.

With typical bombast in his criticism, Shaw feverishly and frequently desecrated that most venerated of British institutions:

> There are moments when one asks despairingly why our stage should ever have been cursed with this 'immortal' pilferer of other men's stories and ideas, with his monstrous rhetorical fustian, his unbearable platitudes, his pretentious reduction of the subtlest problems of life to commonplaces against which a Polytechnic debating club would revolt, his incredible unsuggestiveness, his sententious combination of ready reflection with complete intellectual sterility, and his consequent incapacity for getting out of the depth of even the most ignorant audience....There is no eminent writer, not even Sir Walter Scott, whom I can despise so entirely as I despise Shakespeare when I measure my mind against his. The intensity of my impatience with him occasionally reaches such a pitch, that it would positively be a relief to me to dig him up and throw stones at him, knowing as I do how incapable he and his worshippers are of understanding any less obvious form of indignity.

Shaw also carried his campaign into his playwriting. *Caesar and Cleopatra* pits itself against both *Julius Caesar* and *Antony and Cleopatra*, its central figure deliberately construed not as a tyrant or a romantic lover and soldier but a clear-sighted, cultured Shavian realist and, according to Shaw, 'an improvement on Shakespear's'. In *Cymbeline Refinished* (1936) Shaw boldly purports to 'fix' the final act of Shakespeare's romance, correcting what he described as 'a tedious string of unsurprising *denouements* sugared with insincere sentimentality after a ludicrous stage battle'. In its place, Shaw devises a conclusion 'as Shakespear might have written it if he had been post-Ibsen and post-Shaw'.

At the same time, though, he admired Shakespeare's dramaturgical skill immensely, claiming to have known the plays from a very young age. 'Shakespeare', he wrote, 'as far as sonority, imagery, wit, humor, energy of imagination, power over language, and a whimsically keen eye for idiosyncrasies can make a dramatist, was the king of dramatists.' In addition to frequently praising his dramatic structure, Shaw felt Shakespeare's poetic genius most visible in his 'word-music':

> There is a great deal of feeling, highly poetic and highly dramatic, which cannot be expressed by mere words—because words are the counters of thinking, not of feeling—but which can be supremely expressed by music. The poet tries to make his words serve his purpose by arranging them musically.

The danger, for Shaw, with regard to this richness in the language, besides the potential obscuring of intellectual ideas, is that it could harmonize spectators into complicity with Shakespeare's scepticism about human nature. Nonetheless, he situated his own innovations with stage dialogue within the same genealogy. Looking over his own plays, he wrote in 1933 that,

> in a generation which knew nothing of any sort of acting but drawing room comedy, and which considered a speech of more than twenty words impossibly long, I went back to the classical style and wrote long rhetorical speeches like operatic solos, regarding my plays as musical performances precisely as Shakespear did.... Yet so novel was my post-Marx post-Ibsen outlook on life that nobody suspected that my methods were as old as the stage itself.

Not surprising then that, in 1910, he wrote a short playlet entitled *The Dark Lady of the Sonnets* 'for a performance in aid of the funds of the project for establishing a National Theatre as a memorial to Shakespeare'.

The other part of his dispute with Shakespeare had less to do with the playwright and more with how his plays were decimated on the Victorian stage to appease the wishes of audiences and theatre practitioners alike. Always infuriated at any short-circuiting of critical thinking, he abhorred the blind worshipping of Shakespeare, a phenomenon which he termed 'Bardolatry'. He faulted the actor-manager system for ego-driven cutting of scripts and prioritizing period design elements over the thematic and structural integrity of the plays.

Shaw further railed against the ways in which actors within these spectacles chewed scenery in performance, over-emphasized sentiment, and betrayed the 'on the line and to the line' style of playing that he felt Shakespeare's language demanded, 'with the utterance and acting simultaneous, inseparable and in fact identical'. He vigorously supported companies such as the Elizabethan Stage Society as well as Harley Granville-Barker's minimalist stagings of the plays *as written* that foregrounded the language above all.

His disagreements with his predecessor's outlook on humanity aside, Shaw's relentless attack on Shakespeare was part of his larger critique of the 19th-century theatre and one that he maintained was quite successful. In his final essay for the *Saturday Review*, he claimed that, 'when I began to write, William was a divinity and a bore. Now he is a fellow-creature.' The preface to *Three Plays for Puritans* declares a decisive victory in purging stage inanities:

> It was the age of gross ignorance of Shakespear and incapacity for
> his works that produced the indiscriminate eulogies with which we

are familiar. It was the revival of serious attention to those works that coincided with the movement for giving genuine instead of spurious and silly representations of his plays. So much for Bardolatry!

Shakes versus Shav (1949)

Quite fittingly, then, Shaw returns to his quarrel with Shakespeare in what he considers in all 'actuarial probability' to be his 'last play' and 'the climax of [his] eminence'. The eccentric, rarely performed *Shakes versus Shav*, written nearly half a century after his criticism, supplies the most moving and revealing coda to his unusually long career and even longer life. It is written in the style of 'Punch and Judy', envisioning Shakespeare and Shaw as bickering puppets, railing at one another and each coming to terms with the loss of control over their work that mortality imposes. His invoking of Commedia conventions in this short work gestures to his branding of GBS, which he understood within the context of those archetypes: 'It was as Punch that I emerged from obscurity...to be the most humourously extravagant paradoxer in London.' Using this idiom is also a cheeky nod to the view held by some critics that Shaw's dramaturgy was such a regime, his characters, as one of them in his comedy *Fanny's First Play* (1911) asserts, 'are himself: mere puppets stuck up to spout Shaw'.

In *Shakes versus Shav*, Shakes enters first, ranting against the upstart crow Shav whom he calls a 'shameless fraud' and an 'infamous imposter' possessed by an 'ecstasy of self-conceit' in '[daring] to pretend here to reincarnate my very self'. Shav soon emerges, every bit the aggressive bounder, and, predictably, they brawl and grouse at one another, trading accusations of pessimism and plagiarism even as the plucky younger playwright proclaims *Heartbreak House* every inch equal to *King Lear*. The characters' rivalry notwithstanding, the culminating effect of the play is to see them as peers, the two greatest playwrights in the English language struggling with the insecurities of both canonization and posterity, both, in the end, inescapably Time's puppets. What begins as an ego-driven contest over creative greatness concludes at a reckoning with the transience of individual existence. Shav asks Shakes to 'for a moment suffer | My glimmering light to shine.' When a light suddenly and mysteriously appears between them, Shakes responds by 'puffing [it] out' and saying 'out, out brief candle'. The resultant darkness vanquishes both figures in an abrupt, uncertain conclusion replete with equal potential for despair and optimism but providing no clear confirmation of evolutionary progress, similar to the end of *Too True to Be Good*.

In a 1907 speech, Shaw shared:

> I am of the opinion that my life belongs to the community, and as long as I live, it is my privilege to do for it whatever I can. I want to be thoroughly used up when I die, for the harder I work, the more I live. Life is no 'brief candle' to me. It is a sort of splendid torch which I have got hold of for a moment, and I want to make it burn as brightly as possible before handing it on to the future generations.

Asked in an interview when he was 70 if he felt himself a good model of *Methuselah*'s long livers, the playwright responded: 'I can imagine nothing more dreadful than an eternity of Bernard Shaw.' According to the preface to *Three Plays for Puritans*, in order to mean something, notoriety must be, like theatre, ephemeral:

> Reputations are cheap nowadays. Even were they dear, it would still be impossible for any public-spirited citizen of the world to hope that his reputation might endure; for this would be to hope that the flood of general enlightenment may never rise above his miserable high-watermark.... We must hurry on: we must get rid of reputations: they are weeds in the soil of ignorance. Cultivate that soil, and they will flower more beautifully, but only as annuals.

Along the same lines, late in *Shakes versus Shav*, Shav sets forth
an expansive vision, itself a pastiche of repurposed lines from
three Shakespeare plays:

> Tomorrow and tomorrow and tomorrow
> We puppets shall replay our scene. Meanwhile,
> Immortal William dead and turned to clay
> May stop a hole to keep the wind away.

Lacking Macbeth's sense of sterile futility, Shav's far-reaching
'tomorrows' suggest that both the advancement of the drama as
well as the general deepening of thought, spirit, and organization
depend upon the endless replaying of the puppets' scene. Its
essence is the animating principle of Shaw's work as an artist and
public intellectual: *contention*.

From the calculated generation of friction between sparring
perspectives, beliefs, and values come the sparks of progress,
forged within the smithy of discussion. Shaw never shies away
from the complexities of the subjects he tackles; as Eric Bentley
put it, on most questions, 'Shaw's answer was not Either/Or but
Both/And', striving towards creative synthesis within the interplay
of competing viewpoints. As is often pointed out, there are no true
villains in Shaw plays; articulate, reasonable, and properly
weighted (even if the playwright sometimes puckishly tips the
scales in favour of the devil's advocates), every character's position
is essential to the fecundity of the discussion. As he made clear in
The Quintessence of Ibsenism, the real pitfalls are rigid idealism,
stubborn dogmatism, and beliefs severed from their connection to
the world and from perpetual engagement with their
counterpoints.

While Shav embodies his anti-establishment exuberance, Shaw, by
this time, has just as much in common with the outraged Shakes,
GBS having been a fully-fledged national institution for decades.

What he had witnessed with Shakespeare's plays on the 19th-century stage made clear what could happen to a writer's work when he wasn't around to protect it. He called Henry Irving's *Cymbeline* a 'disemboweling' and more generally described the stage adaptation of Shakespeare's works in the late 19th century as a process 'of debasement and mutilation', an 'extremity of misrepresentation' from which only the 'living author can protect himself'. His published prefaces and extensive stage directions could only go so far in ensuring the integrity of his dramaturgical vision and safeguarding against the garbling of Shavianism in the future. Even so, he understands that social and artistic evolution depends upon the challenging of the establishment. It is the obligation of rising generations to decry their predecessors and modify their legacies: 'It's all the young can do for the old,' Shaw wrote in *Fanny's First Play*, 'to shock them and keep them up to date.'

In the preface to *Three Plays for Puritans*, written in 1900, Shaw muses about his ability to 'so transfigure the eternal stage puppets and their inevitable dilemmas' as to appear momentarily novel:

> I shall perhaps enjoy a few years of immortality. But the whirligig of time will soon bring my audiences to my own point of view; and then the next Shakespear that comes along will turn these pretty tentatives of mine into masterpieces for their epoch. By that time, my twentieth century characteristics will pass unnoticed as a matter of course, whilst the eighteenth century artificiality of every literary Irishman of my generation will seem antiquated and silly.

His vision of fertile advancement is one in which his words and ideas become antiquated and useless; once the rest of the world catches up to GBS, it must then leave him behind, progressing towards higher planes of human existence. As he predicted in 1900, new generations of playwrights began to arise and sought to establish themselves by pushing back against the authority of their forebears, as he did with Shakespeare. But much still endures through the wrangling. From the cultivated linguistic styles of Noël Coward and Harold Pinter to the 'state of the nation' plays of John Osborne and David Hare to the stage extravaganzas of Tony Kushner, Caryl Churchill, and Tom Stoppard, the Shavian inheritance is clear; regardless of to what degree individual playwrights embraced or challenged it, his role in the creative evolution of modern and contemporary drama was profound and farfetched.

In the 1944 revised preface to *Back to Methuselah*, Shaw reflectively shared at length his understanding of what he called 'My Own Part in the Matter':

> The worst convention of the criticism of the theatre current at that time was that intellectual seriousness is out of place on the stage; that the theatre is a place of shallow amusement; that people go there to be soothed after the enormous intellectual strain of a day in the city: in short, that a playwright is a person whose business it is to make unwholesome confectionery out of cheap emotions....
>
> In my own activities as a playwright I found this state of things intolerable.... I tried slum-landlordism, doctrinaire Free Love (pseudo-Ibsenism), prostitution, militarism, marriage, history, current politics, natural Christianity, national and individual character, paradoxes of conventional society, husband hunting, questions of conscience, professional delusions and impostures, all worked into a series of comedies of manners in the classic fashion, which was then very much out of fashion, the mechanical tricks of Parisian 'construction' being de rigueur in the theatre....
>
> [Now] my powers are waning; but so much the better for those who found me unbearably brilliant when I was in my prime. It is my hope that a hundred apter and more elegant parables by younger hands will soon leave mine as far behind as the religious pictures of the fifteenth century left behind the first attempts of the early Christians at iconography. In that hope I withdraw and ring up the curtain.

In that same hope is placed the blackout that ends *Shakes versus Shav*.

In the preface to his last full-length play *Buoyant Billions*, Shaw returns to the same subject, taking a decidedly more mystical approach to his playwriting in which particularized motive and personal agency are transcended:

> There is nothing in my circumstances or personality to suggest that I differ from any other son of a downstart gentleman driven by lack of unearned income to become an incompetent merchant and harp on his gentility.... When I write a play, I do not foresee nor intend a page of it from one end to the other; the play writes itself. I may reason out every sentence until I have made it say exactly what it comes to me to say, but whence and how and why it comes to me,... I do not know.

He draws an analogy between his writing self and that of a Spiritualist medium, 'in whose hands a pencil of any sort will, apparently of its own volition, write communications undreamt-of by the medium'. While his 'readers keep complaining' that he has 'not solved all the problems of the universe for them', Shaw here humbly represents himself as 'obviously neither omnipotent, omniscient, nor infallible' and as being 'not a god nor even the proprietor of The Times (as they all assume)'. Somewhere lurking behind such statements is John Tanner's anguished cry at the end of *Man and Superman*: 'The Life Force. I am in the grip of the Life Force.'

Since his death and into this new century of unprecedented digitized access to worldwide resources old and new, Bernard Shaw's writings persist as his (and the Life Force's) evangelical instruments, continuing to challenge the orthodoxies of our thinking in the face of ongoing social injustice, increasing global instability, and chronic violence. Like Tanner, he has kept on talking. And we have continued to listen, respond, and discuss.

In classrooms. In theatres. In popular culture. GBS continues to engross and provoke, even as his ideas adapt to new political contexts, his words to new artistic trends, his message to new proliferative platforms. With his 'discussion drama' as well as his journalism, the cornerstone of Shaw's model remains resolutely Fabian—a sustained investment in committed conversation and creative collaboration among all stakeholders, especially those with perspectives that diverge from one's own. Besides his impressive and extensive body of written work, Shaw's faith in robust intellectual contention is indeed what endures, his belief that true reform and progress proceed from the meaningful collisions of ideas with their alternatives across all media. Overall, for Shaw, the thing's the play.

Chronology of Shaw's major writings

1856	Born in Dublin (26 July)
1876	Moves to London
1879–83	Novels: *Immaturity*, *The Irrational Knot*, *Love Among the Artists*, *Cashel Byron's Profession*, and *An Unsocial Socialist*
1884	Joins the Fabian Society
1885–98	Writes art, music, fiction, and theatre criticism
1888	Whitechapel murders by Jack the Ripper
1891	*The Quintessence of Ibsenism*
1892	*Widower's Houses*
1893	*The Philanderer* and *Mrs Warren's Profession*
1894	*Arms and the Man* and *Candida*
1895	*The Man of Destiny*
1896	*You Never Can Tell* and *The Devil's Disciple*
1898	*Caesar and Cleopatra* and *The Perfect Wagnerite*
	Marries Charlotte Payne-Townshend
	Publishes *Plays Pleasant and Unpleasant*
1901	Publishes *Three Plays for Puritans*
	Queen Victoria dies and accession of Edward VII
1902	*Man and Superman*

1904–7	Royal Court Theatre with Harley Granville-Barker
1905	*Major Barbara*
1906	*The Doctor's Dilemma*
1908	*Getting Married*
1909	*Misalliance*
1911	*Fanny's First Play*
1912	*Pygmalion*
	The sinking of the *Titanic*
1914–18	First World War
1914	*Common Sense About the War*
1915	*O'Flaherty V.C.*
1916	Easter Rising in Dublin
1917	*Heartbreak House*
1920	*Back to Methuselah*
	League of Nations formed as part of Treaty of Versailles
1923	*Saint Joan*
1925	First public performance of *Mrs Warren's Profession* in England
1926	Awarded the 1925 Nobel Prize for Literature
1928	*The Intelligent Woman's Guide to Socialism and Capitalism* and *The Apple Cart*
	Women in Britain granted the right to vote
1929	Stock market crashes, causing worldwide economic depression
1931	GBS tours Soviet Russia
	Too True to Be Good
1933	*On the Rocks*
	Adolf Hitler appointed Chancellor of Germany
1934	*The Simpleton of the Unexpected Isles*
1935	*The Millionairess*
1936	*Geneva*

1939–45	Second World War
1939	Wins Academy Award for his *Pygmalion* screenplay
1943	Charlotte dies
1944	*Everybody's Political What's What*
1945–51	Labour government and the creation of the 'welfare state'
1946	*Buoyant Billions*
1948	*Farfetched Fables*
1949	*Shakes versus Shav*
1950	Dies (2 November) in Ayot St Lawrence, Hertfordshire

References

Quotes from plays and prefaces in this book are from *The Bodley Head Bernard Shaw: Collected Plays with their Prefaces*, 7 volumes (London: The Bodley Head, 1970–4). Quotes from Shaw's criticism are taken from *Our Theatres in the Nineties*, 3 volumes (New York: W. M. H. Wise & Company, 1931). Dates are keyed to A. M. Gibbs's *A Bernard Shaw Chronology* (New York: Palgrave, 2001).

Introduction: 'Shavian'

Fintan O'Toole, *Judging Shaw: The Radicalism of GBS* (Dublin: Prism, 2017), 4, 22.

J. B. Priestley, 'Thoughts on Shaw', *New Statesman and Nation* (28 July 1956).

Chapter 1: 'GBS'

Maurice Colbourne, *The Real Bernard Shaw* (New York: Dodd, Mead & Company, 1940), 73.

Archibald Henderson, *George Bernard Shaw: His Life and Works, a Critical Biography* (Cincinnati: Stewart & Kidd Company, 1911), 503.

Nelson O'Ceallaigh Ritschel, *Bernard Shaw, W. T. Stead, and the New Journalism* (London: Palgrave Macmillan, 2017), 219.

Chapter 2: 'Unpleasant'

L. W. Conolly, ed., 'Introduction'. In George Bernard Shaw, *Mrs Warren's Profession*, ed. L. W. Conolly (Peterborough, Canada: Broadview Press, 2005), 55.

Michael Holroyd, *Bernard Shaw: The One Volume Definitive Edition* (New York: Random House, 1997), 235.

Gilbert Murray, *Aristophanes: A Study* (Oxford: Clarendon Press, 1933), Dedication.

Chapter 3: 'Pleasant'

Bertolt Brecht's statement is quoted from Michael Holroyd, *Bernard Shaw: The Pursuit of Power (1898–1918)*, volume 2 (New York: Random House, 1989), 247.

A. M. Gibbs, 'Bernard Shaw's Family Skeletons: A New Look', *Bullán: An Irish Studies Journal* 3:1 (Spring 1997): 57–74, 69.

Chapter 4: 'Puritan'

G. K. Chesterton, *George Bernard Shaw* (New York: John Lane Company, 1909), 46–7.

A. M. Gibbs, *Bernard Shaw: A Life* (Gainesville: University of Florida Press, 2005), 232.

Chapter 5: 'Political'

John Barnes, 'Tropics of a Desirable Oxymoron: The Radical Superman in *Back to Methuselah*', *SHAW: The Annual of Bernard Shaw Studies* 17 (1997), ed. Milton T. Wolf (The Pennsylvania State University Press, 1997): 155–64, 161.

Eric Bentley, *Bernard Shaw* (New York: Applause Books, 2002), 161.

Ronald Bryden, *Shaw and his Contemporaries: Theatre Essays* (Oakville, Ontario: Mosaic Press, 2003), 42.

Peter Gahan, *Shaw Shadows: Rereading the Texts of Bernard Shaw* (Gainesville: University of Florida Press, 2004), 194.

A. M. Gibbs, *Bernard Shaw: A Life* (Gainesville: University of Florida Press, 2005), 431.

Nelson O'Ceallaigh Ritschel, *Bernard Shaw, W. T. Stead, and the New Journalism* (London: Palgrave Macmillan, 2017), 193.

Chapter 6: 'Extravagant'

Ronald Bryden, *Shaw and his Contemporaries: Theatre Essays* (Oakville, Ontario: Mosaic Press, 2003), 11.

Richard Farr Dietrich, 'Novels', *George Bernard Shaw in Context*, ed. Brad Kent (Cambridge: Cambridge University Press, 2015), 168–74, 168.

Margery Morgan, *The Shavian Playground: An Exploration of the Art of George Bernard Shaw* (London: Methuen, 1972), 327.

Matthew Yde, *Bernard Shaw and Totalitarianism: Longing for Utopia* (London: Palgrave Macmillan, 2013), 6.

Chapter 7: 'Farfetched'

Eric Bentley, *Bernard Shaw* (New York: Applause Books, 2002), 232.

Sally Peters, *Bernard Shaw: The Ascent of the Superman* (New Haven: Yale University Press, 1996), 258.

Further reading

Annotated editions of Shaw's plays

Bernard Shaw, *The Philanderer*, ed. L. W. Conolly (Peterborough, Canada: Broadview Press, 2005).

Bernard Shaw, *Mrs Warren's Profession*, ed. L. W. Conolly (Peterborough, Canada: Broadview Press, 2005).

Bernard Shaw, *Arms and the Man*, ed. J. P. Wearing (London: Methuen, 2008).

Bernard Shaw, *Major Barbara*, ed. Nicholas Grene (London: Methuen, 2008).

Bernard Shaw, *Mrs Warren's Profession*, ed. Brad Kent (London: Methuen, 2008).

Bernard Shaw, *Pygmalion*, ed. L. W. Conolly (London: Methuen, 2008).

Bernard Shaw, *Saint Joan*, ed. Jean Chothia (London: Methuen, 2008).

Bernard Shaw, *The Apple Cart, On the Rocks, Too True to Be Good, The Millionairess*, ed. Matthew Yde (Oxford: Oxford University Press, 2021).

Bernard Shaw, *Arms and the Man, The Devil's Disciple, Caesar and Cleopatra*, ed. Lawrence Switzky (Oxford: Oxford University Press, 2021).

Bernard Shaw, *Man and Superman, John Bull's Other Island, Major Barbara,* ed. Brad Kent (Oxford: Oxford University Press, 2021).

Bernard Shaw, *Mrs Warren's Profession, Candida, You Never Can Tell*, ed. Sos Eltis (Oxford: Oxford University Press, 2021).

Bernard Shaw, *Playlets* (Shorter Plays), ed. James Moran (Oxford: Oxford University Press, 2021).

Bernard Shaw, *Pygmalion, Heartbreak House, Saint Joan*, ed. Brad
    Kent (Oxford: Oxford University Press, 2021).

Annotated editions of other writing by Shaw

Bernard Shaw, *Major Cultural Essays*, ed. David Kornhaber (Oxford:
    Oxford University Press, 2021).
Bernard Shaw, *Major Political Writings*, ed. Elizabeth Carolyn Miller
    (Oxford: Oxford University Press, 2021).
Bernard F. Dukore, ed., *The Collected Screenplays of Bernard Shaw*
    (Athens: University of Georgia Press, 1980).
Dan H. Laurence, ed., *Bernard Shaw: Collected Letters*, 3 volumes
    (New York: Viking, 1965–85).
Bernard Shaw, *The Intelligent Woman's Guide to Socialism,
    Capitalism, Sovietism, and Fascism* (London: Alma, 2012).
Edwin Wilson, ed., *Shaw on Shakespeare* (New York: Applause Books,
    1961).
J. L. Wisenthal, ed., *Shaw and Ibsen. Bernard Shaw's 'The
    Quintessence of Ibsenism' and Related Writings* (Toronto:
    University of Toronto Press, 1979).
J. L. Wisenthal and Daniel O'Leary, eds, *What Shaw Really Wrote
    About the War* (Gainesville: University of Florida Press, 2006).
One of the challenges involved in writing a volume of this size was
    how much had to be left out, especially about a life and career that
    spanned nearly a century and a man who penned (according to
    conservative estimates) a quarter of a million letters and postcards
    alone in addition to his large body of published writings. Luckily,
    there is a robust critical conversation about Shaw and his work to
    texture and complicate this brief introduction. For decades,
    SHAW: The Journal of Bernard Shaw Studies (published with
    Penn State University Press) has provided a forum for the
    exchange of ideas about the man and his writing. For more
    extended studies, the following are suggestions for places to begin
    further reading:

Books about Shaw

A. M. Gibbs, *Bernard Shaw: A Life* (Gainesville: University of Florida
    Press, 2005).
Michael Holroyd, *Bernard Shaw: The One Volume Definitive Edition*
    (New York: Random House, 1997).

Fintan O'Toole, *Judging Shaw: The Radicalism of GBS* (Dublin: Prism, 2017).

Sally Peters, *Bernard Shaw: The Ascent of the Superman* (New Haven: Yale University Press, 1996).

Stanley Weintraub, *Bernard Shaw 1914–1918: Journey to Heartbreak* (London: Routledge & Kegan Paul, 1973).

Stanley Weintraub, *Shaw's People: Victoria to Churchill* (University Park, Pa: Penn State University Press, 1996).

Books about Shaw's writing

Eric Bentley, *Bernard Shaw* (New York: Applause Books, 2002).

John Bertolini, *The Playwrighting Self of Bernard Shaw* (Carbondale: Southern Illinois University Press, 1991).

Ronald Bryden, *Shaw and his Contemporaries: Theatre Essays* (Oakville, Ontario: Mosaic Press, 2003).

David Clare, *Bernard Shaw's Irish Outlook* (London: Palgrave Macmillan, 2016).

L. W. Conolly, *Bernard Shaw and the BBC* (Toronto: University of Toronto Press, 2009).

Tracy C. Davis, *George Bernard Shaw and the Socialist Theatre* (New York: Praeger, 1994).

Richard Farr Dietrich, *Bernard Shaw's Novels: Portraits of the Artist as Man and Superman* (Gainesville: University of Florida Press, 1996).

Bernard Dukore, *Shaw's Theater* (Gainesville: University of Florida Press, 2000).

Bernard Dukore, *Crimes and Punishments and Bernard Shaw* (London: Palgrave Macmillan, 2017).

Peter Gahan, *Bernard Shaw and Beatrice Webb on Poverty and Equality in the Modern World, 1905–1914* (London: Palgrave Macmillan, 2017).

R. A. Gaines, ed., *Bernard Shaw's Marriages and Misalliances* (London: Palgrave Macmillan, 2017).

J. Ellen Gainor, *Shaw's Daughters: Dramatic and Narrative Constructions of Gender* (Ann Arbor: The University of Michigan Press, 1991).

D. A. Hadfield and Jean Reynolds, eds, *Shaw and Feminisms: On Stage and Off* (Gainesville: University of Florida Press, 2016).

Christopher Innes, ed., *The Cambridge Companion to George Bernard Shaw* (Cambridge: Cambridge University Press, 1998).

Brad Kent, ed., *George Bernard Shaw in Context* (Cambridge: Cambridge University Press, 2015).

Martin Miesel, *Shaw and the Nineteenth-Century Theater* (Westport, Conn.: Greenwood, 1976).

Margery Morgan, *The Shavian Playground: An Exploration of the Art of George Bernard Shaw* (London: Methuen, 1972).

Jean Reynolds, *Pygmalion's Wordplay: The Postmodern Shaw* (Gainesville: University of Florida Press, 1999).

Nelson O'Ceallaigh Ritschel, *Bernard Shaw, W. T. Stead, and the New Journalism* (London: Palgrave Macmillan, 2017).

Joan Templeton, *Shaw's Ibsen* (London: Palgrave Macmillan, 2018).

Rodelle Weintraub, *Fabian Feminist: Bernard Shaw and Women* (University Park, Pa: Penn State University Press, 1977).

Matthew Yde, *Bernard Shaw and Totalitarianism: Longing for Utopia* (London: Palgrave Macmillan, 2013).

Online Shaw

The Shaw Society (UK): <shawsociety.org.uk/and on Twitter @ ShawSoc>.

The International Shaw Society: <shawsociety.org>.

YouTube GBS channel: <youtube.com/channel/UCxGpZjHhix37VN-zFfX6psg/playlists>.

Index

For the benefit of digital users, indexed terms that span two pages (e.g., 52–53) may, on occasion, appear on only one of those pages.

BESTSELLERS
A Very Short Introduction
John Sutherland

'I rejoice', said Doctor Johnson, 'to concur with the Common Reader.' For the last century, the tastes and preferences of the common reader have been reflected in the American and British bestseller lists, and this *Very Short Introduction* takes an engaging look through the lists to reveal what we have been reading - and why. John Sutherland shows that bestseller lists monitor one of the strongest pulses in modern literature and are therefore worthy of serious study. Along the way, he lifts the lid on the bestseller industry, examines what makes a book into a bestseller, and asks what separates bestsellers from canonical fiction.

> 'His amiable trawl through the history of popular books is frequently entertaining'
>
> **Scott Pack, The Times**

BIOGRAPHY
A Very Short Introduction
Hermione Lee

Biography is one of the most popular, best-selling, and widely-read of literary genres. But why do certain people and historical events arouse so much interest? How can biographies be compared with history and works of fiction? Does a biography need to be true? Is it acceptable to omit or conceal things? Does the biographer need to personally know the subject? Must a biographer be subjective? In this *Very Short Introduction* Hermione Lee considers the cultural and historical background of different types of biographies, looking at the factors that affect biographers and whether there are different strategies, ethics, and principles required for writing about one person compared to another. She also considers contemporary biographical publications and considers what kind of 'lives' are the most popular and in demand.

'It would be hard to think of anyone better to provide a crisp contribution to OUP's Very Short Introductions.'

Kathryn Hughes, The Guardian

ENGLISH LITERATURE
A Very Short Introduction
Jonathan Bate

Sweeping across two millennia and every literary genre, acclaimed scholar and biographer Jonathan Bate provides a dazzling introduction to English Literature. The focus is wide, shifting from the birth of the novel and the brilliance of English comedy to the deep Englishness of landscape poetry and the ethnic diversity of Britain's Nobel literature laureates. It goes on to provide a more in-depth analysis, with close readings from an extraordinary scene in King Lear to a war poem by Carol Ann Duffy, and a series of striking examples of how literary texts change as they are transmitted from writer to reader.

{No reviews}